Wrapped

by Dr. Randy T. Johnson

with contributions by:

Roger Allen
Noble Baird
Christopher Blodgett
Holly Boston
Jared Bruder
Isaiah Combs
Brett Eberle
Jeff England
Bryan Fox
Debbie Gabbara
Eric Jeffrey
Scott Johnson

Debbie Kerr
William Kinney
Chuck Lindsey
Lorna Lyman
Pat MacDermaid
Wes McCullough
Philip Piasecki
John Sanchez
Ryan Story
Katrina Young
Michael Young
Dave Zidel

First Edition, November 2016

Published by:
The River Church
8393 E. Holly Rd.
Holly, MI 48442

Scriptures are taken from the Bible,
English Standard Version (ESV)

THE RIVER CHURCH

Printed in the United States of America

CONTENTS

WEEK 1: God's Promises

WEEK 2: God's Plan

WEEK 3: God's Purpose

WEEK 7: *Gather*

WEEK 8: *Grow*

WEEK 9: *Back to Reach*

1

God's Promises

Philip Piasecki | Worship Leader

O
n April 27, 2016, God blessed Mary and me with our first child. After going twelve days past her due date, Molly Grace Piasecki was finally born, and our whole world changed. People tried to explain to me what the feeling would be like to have your first child, but I could never have imagined I could love her as much as I do. Sometimes I will just stare at her and wish I could promise her the whole world. The crazy thing is, as much as I love my daughter, God loves her infinitely more. He loves each and every one of us in a way we cannot even comprehend. Throughout Scripture, He makes countless promises to His children. When we make promises to those that we love, sometimes we will break those promises. However, God will never break the promises He makes to us. The things that have been promised to us in the Scripture will be or already have been fulfilled. There are over 3,000 promises in Scripture, and I wish we had time to look at each one of them in this lesson!

In your life, what is the most memorable promise you have ever made and followed through? _____

_____

_____

_____

Isaiah 7:14 says, *"Therefore the Lord himself will give you a sign. Behold, the virgin shall conceive and bear a son, and shall call his name Immanuel."*

Matthew 1:20-23 adds, *"But as he considered these things, behold, an angel of the Lord appeared to him in a dream, saying, 'Joseph, son of David, do not fear to take Mary as your wife, for that which is conceived in her is from the Holy Spirit. She will bear a son, and you shall call his name Jesus, for he will save his people from their sins.' All this took place to fulfill what the Lord had spoken by the prophet:*

'Behold, the virgin shall conceive and bear a son,
and they shall call his name Immanuel' (which means, God with us)."

What promises are found in these verses and why are they significant? _____

_____
_____
_____

How do you think Joseph felt hearing this promise? What would your reaction have been? _____

_____
_____
_____

We see in Isaiah 7:14 that God promised He would send His Son. In Matthew 1:20-23 we see the promise that Jesus will save His people from their sins. Both of these promises are so significant because they made a way for us to be saved from our sins. Without the birth of Christ, He never would have been able to be crucified, buried, and rise again. The fulfillment of the promise of Christ's birth paved the way for the promise of salvation.

Deuteronomy 4:29: *"But from there you will seek the Lord your God and you will find him, if you search after him with all your heart and with all your soul."*

1 John 1:9: *"If we confess our sins, he is faithful and just to forgive us our sins and to cleanse us from all unrighteousness."*

Acts 2:21: *"And it shall come to pass that everyone who calls upon the name of the Lord shall be saved."*

Romans 10:9: *"Because, if you confess with your mouth that Jesus is Lord and believe in your heart that God raised him from the dead, you will be saved."*

What are the common themes in each of these verses?

_____
_____
_____

What is your testimony of salvation? _____

_____
_____
_____
_____

Of all the promises God makes in Scripture, the promise of salvation is the most important. Scripture makes it very clear that if we confess our sin, believe in the resurrection, and turn to Christ, He WILL save us. We do not have to be unsure about our salvation at any point in our life if we have done these things. There will still be times when we stumble; the Christian life can be a tough battle. When we stumble, we can rest in the promise of our salvation. All of the other promises of God are important, but if we have not fully understood the promise of salvation, then they mean nothing. Once we know that we have fully given our lives to Christ, we can rejoice in the many other promises of God.

Philippians 4:19: *"And my God will supply every need of yours according to his riches in glory in Christ Jesus."*

Matthew 6:25-33: *"Therefore I tell you, do not be anxious about your life, what you will eat or what you will drink, nor about your body, what you will put on. Is not life more than food, and the body more than clothing? Look at the birds of the air: they neither sow nor reap nor gather into barns, and yet your heavenly Father feeds them. Are you not of more value than they? And which of you by being anxious can add a single hour to his span of life? And why are you anxious about clothing? Consider the lilies of the field, how they grow: they neither toil nor spin, yet I tell you, even Solomon in all his glory was not arrayed like one of these. But if God so clothes the grass of the field, which today is alive and tomorrow is thrown into the oven, will he not much more clothe you, O you of little faith? Therefore do not be anxious, saying, 'What shall we eat?' or 'What shall we drink?' or 'What shall we wear?' For the Gentiles seek after all these things, and your heavenly Father knows that you need them all. But seek first the kingdom of God and his righteousness, and all these things will be added to you."*

What are the "needs" that God promises to supply?

_____

_____

_____

What do you think *"according to His riches in glory in Jesus Christ"* means in Philippians 4:19? _____

_____

_____

How does Jesus encourage us not to worry in Matthew 6:25-33?

_____

_____

_____

God has promised to supply our every need. To fully understand this we need to adjust our perception of what is actually a need. In America, we have been blessed with so much. There are so many things that we have that we would consider essential to living. I am sure the majority of us could never imagine living without our cell phones. However, it was just a few years ago that they did not exist at all! When we comprehend how much we have that is not essential to living, we can better understand God promising to provide our every need. The phrase *"according to His riches in Glory in Jesus Christ"* explains to us that God made a way to supply our every need through Jesus Christ. The idea that this is done *"in Glory"* is the Scriptures way of explaining that God providing for us is done in a glorious manner. God does not do anything that is not worthy of Himself. All of His actions are done in a manner that brings praise and glory to Himself. Jesus tells us to think of the birds in the air and the lilies in the field. Jesus explains that if God takes care of them, of course He is going to provide for us because He loves us so much more than the grass and the birds! God promises that He will provide for us, He provides for our eternal needs, and He will also provide for our physical needs.

In what situations do you find yourself doubting the provision of God the most? _____

_____

_____

What can you do to refocus and better trust in the promise of God to provide for you? _____

_____

_____

The Scripture is packed full of the promises of God. I would challenge you to do a study of all the different promises that are made in Scripture. First and foremost God promised He would send His Son to save us from our sins. Jesus' sacrifice on the cross made a way for us to secure eternal life. God promises salvation to those who repent of their sins and believe in Jesus Christ. As Christians, we never have to doubt that we will actually be in Heaven with Christ one day. God promises to provide our needs as well. We need to understand that our desires and needs are two very different things. God may not say yes to that prayer for a new sports car, but when we seek Him, He will supply our every need. In times of want, we need to trust in God that He has provided us with everything we need at that moment. My prayer is that we can be people that trust God for our salvation, trust Him to provide for us, and share the love of Christ to all those who need it.

THE PROMISES OF GOD

Eric Jeffrey | Children's Director

I magine a world where every product ever advertised did exactly what it promised. Imagine if everyone that promised to do something actually did what he or she promised; I can only imagine because it just does not happen. Money promises happiness, technology promises life easier, and power promises joy. If this were a true statement, then this world would not need God and the Savior, but it clearly does because the promises the world has to offer cannot compare to the promises of God.

The Bible is like a treasure chest, but instead of gold, it is full of the promises of God. Sadly, many Christians do not know God's promises, and we never open it to see what inside. However, God wants us to open this treasure chest and see all the riches we have in His promises. He wants to reveal His promises to us. He wants us to trust his promises and be transformed by His promises. We can only do that if we know His promises. So, what are the promises of God?

Eternal Life – *"That if thou shalt confess with thy mouth the Lord Jesus, and shalt believe in thine heart that God hath raised him from the dead, thou shalt be saved. For with the heart man believeth unto righteousness; and with the mouth confession is made unto salvation"* (Romans 10:9-10 KJV).

Forgiveness – *"If we confess our sins, he is faithful and just to forgive us our sins, and to cleanse us from all unrighteousness"* (1 John 1:9 KJV).

Communion – *"For I am persuaded, that neither death, nor life, nor angels, nor principalities, nor powers, nor things present, nor things to come, Nor height, nor depth, nor any other creature, shall be able to separate us from the love of God, which is in Christ Jesus our Lord"* (Romans 8:38-9 KJV).

Joy- *"And the angel said to them, 'Fear not, for behold, I bring you good news of great joy that will be for all the people'"* (Luke 2:10 KJV).

This is the very short list of God's promises; if you were to add them all up the number would be in the thousands. They are life changing, life giving, and life-sustaining promises free to all who will call upon His name. The thought of God's promises always harkens me to a powerful story in the book of Acts. After the resurrection and ascension of Jesus Christ and the beginning of the church age, Peter and John, Jesus' disciples, went to the temple where they found a lame man that had been this way since birth. The man was begging for money at the entrance to the temple, as was his custom to earn money. It was at this time that Peter and John approached the entrance, and the man asked for a donation. The answer that Peter gave resonates with the nature and power of God's promises. Peter said, "Silver and gold have I none; but such as I have give I thee: In the name of Jesus Christ of Nazareth rise up and walk."

You see, there is no earthly promise that carries the power of God's promises. Sometimes we, me included, put more value and substance to the promises that do not carry the power of God. We sometimes rely on our power to make some promises come true in our lives. In most, if not all cases, we come out on the other end of these worldly promises broken, bitter, and joyless. We sometimes fail to call upon the promises of God like Peter and John did. God promised them power on earth through the Holy Spirit. We can and should stand on God's promises because everything else is like the man that built his house on sand and when the storms came his house was washed away.

READ THE FINE PRINT

Debbie Kerr | Office Administrator

"T*rust in the Lord with all your heart and lean not unto thine own understanding, in all thy ways acknowledge Him and He will direct your path"* (Proverbs 3:5-6 KJV).

When I was a young girl, I remember times my dad would tell me that we might do something fun, such as go to the zoo, circus, or amusement park on Saturday. Saturday would come, and I would be super excited only to discover that there were no plans to go to any of those places. I remember saying to my dad in my whiniest voice, "but you promised." My dad would gently say, "I didn't promise, I said, maybe." You see, my dad did not lie to me or mean to break a promise, he had good intentions, but the circumstances or conditions changed. Maybe the car broke down and the money that we would spend on a family outing had to go to pay for repairs, or someone was sick and the money went to pay the doctor. I began to mistrust or doubt when I heard of a fun idea, but as I grew older and gained understanding, I realized that promises are based on conditions. My dad wanted to give us good things but was not always able because of other factors. Let's face it, sometimes as parents we do break our promises to our children. It is probably best not to make promises, because as humans we cannot see the future. I love the saying, "make your plans in pencil, but give God the pen!"

On the other hand, when God makes a promise, and the appropriate conditions are met, we can always count on Him to deliver. Our Heavenly Father wants to give us good gifts, but the promises He has given us in His Word have conditions attached. One of my favorite verses with a promise is Proverbs 3:5-6. This passage is many people's life verses and often quoted, but I wonder if it is accurately understood and applied.

"Trust in the Lord with ALL thine heart." To trust Him means we believe He only wants the very best for us because He knows the beginning to the end. It might make perfect sense to us at the present, but only He knows the future. Our trust in the Lord, Abba (Daddy) Father has to be greater than our natural desires. We have to know that His love is so much greater than our earthly father who also desires to give us good gifts. It reminds me of the song "Good, Good Father." He loves us so much, and He is perfect in all of His ways. He alone is trustworthy!

"Lean not on our own understanding." This means we need to seek wisdom and counsel from His Word and from godly people that we trust and respect. We cannot trust our own reasoning power when are emotionally attached to an idea or desire. We also need to pray for wisdom. James 1: 5 says, *"If anyone lacks wisdom, let him ask God, who gives generously to all without reproach and it will be given him."* His plan is best even if it seems like the last thing we want.

"In all our ways acknowledge Him." We acknowledge Him by giving Him the preeminence in our lives. We do this by making Him number one; He is Lord over our lives, our desires, dreams, and relationships. We trust Him so much that we know that nothing else will satisfy us, and no one else will cut it for us. When He becomes everything to us, God will not withhold His plan for us when we look to Him for answers. Jeremiah 29: 13 says that God will be found when we search for Him with all our heart. It is when we manipulate, rationalize, or justify our circumstances; we can be assured that we are headed into a storm. It is as if we are saying to God, "I am going to make my plans or follow my

own path, but I want You to bless it." Do you see how backward that is? What we should be praying is, "I surrender to Your plan knowing that You will bless me abundantly for trusting You." We cannot expect God to fulfill His promise of directing our path if we do not do our part.

In my early 20s I talked myself into a situation that I wanted so badly that I ignored Godly wisdom and advice. That was not my nature; it was actually very uncharacteristic for me. The result was devastating, and I entered the six hardest years of my life. The suffering endured by myself and the ones closest to me was brutal, all because I leaned on my own understanding. My foolish thinking hurt many people. No man is an island; there will always be a ripple effect. I repented and sought forgiveness from the ones that were hurt by my foolishness. The beauty of God's amazing grace is that He does not leave us in the mess we have made. He lovingly restored my life and blessed it beyond what I deserved. I still continue to experience the promise of Romans 8:28 that *"God will work ALL things together for good to those who love Him and are the called according to His purpose."* I am thankful He does not give up on us when we make mistakes and miss the mark. His grace and love will always be extravagant when we run back to Him and acknowledge His preeminence in our lives. God redeems and restores according to His promises. There is always hope In Jesus!

PEACE (OR PIECE) OF GOD

Katrina Young | Nursery & Pre-K Director

*"**D**o not be anxious about anything, but in everything by prayer and supplication with thanksgiving let your requests be made known to God. And the peace of God, which surpasses all understanding, will guard your hearts and your minds in Christ Jesus" (Philippians 4:6-7).*

My son was born prematurely twenty-four years ago. We faced all the complications that go along with an early birth, even the possibility of losing him. His path would be an uphill battle of surgeries, therapies, and various medical issues. The normal path of giving birth and the joy that goes with it were gone and replaced with anxiety and fear. I was a fairly new Christian at the time and was beginning to learn God's Word and come to know Him through study. I now had to act on what I had learned through His Word. I had to make a choice to either trust in my God or to allow my emotions and fears control me.

It is natural for anxiety and fear to set in, when we are faced with trials if our hopes are centered on our circumstances, and not in our Heavenly Father and His will for our lives. When our focus is on anyone or anything else, frustration and defeat are inevitable. However, God has promised that, even in the midst of trouble and conflict, if we pray and make our request known to Him, that He will protect our hearts and minds and give us peace.

I learned very quickly that what we were faced with was out of my control. All I could do for my son was pray and put him into God's hands. God already knew my heart, thoughts, and requests. I did not have to tell Him; I needed to trust Him, to act on my faith, and give it to Him. This verse does not express a guarantee that He will give you what you ask for when you pray. It is a promise that if we pray and lay our desires at His feet and trust fully in Him, He will guard our hearts, our minds, and give us peace to face the situation.

We were told over and over what would statistically be our life with our son. God has promised that all things work together for good to those who love and serve Him faithfully (Romans 8:28). He allowed us to see many things through that time that could only be described as miracles. It may be difficult for us to see and understand how this is accomplished at times, but God has promised it through His Word.

No, there is nothing that He cannot do; no situation in our lives is ever beyond His portion of peace to get us through. To help us confidently and boldly trust if we are in His Word, He supplies all our needs.

Psalms 73:26 says, *"My flesh and my heart may fail, but my God is the strength of my heart and my portion forever."*

DEATH WILL DIE

Lorna Lyman | Receptionist

"A *nd we know that for those who love God all things work together for good, for those who are called according to his purpose"* (Romans 8:28).

John and I will celebrate our 25th wedding anniversary this August 17. God has shown Himself to us in many ways during those 25 years. He is with us through the good times and the bad times.

In the early years of our marriage, I was able to finish dental hygiene school. I have been working as a dental hygienist for 22 years now. John was able to go back and finish his degree back in 2011. John and I both love to travel. We have been able to take many trips throughout our married life. We have been blessed with two beautiful girls. We are so thankful they have chosen to follow Christ. They are both saved, have been baptized, and are continuing to grow in their faith.

"For God so loved the world, that he gave his only Son, that whoever believes in him should not perish but have eternal life" (John 3:16).

We have also had some storms that we have had to go through. The first part of our marriage was wonderful. Things were going along quite well. Life was good. Then about nine years into our marriage, we lost John's grandfather. Then a few months later, we lost my grandfather. That was the start of many deaths we would go through the next few years. Death is hard. I am so thankful for God's promise of eternal life to those who believe. I am confident that I will see my loved ones again in heaven someday.   Other storms have come and gone, but all through them God was with us. Growing us closer to Him and believing in His promises.

No matter what is presently going on or what will happen in the future, we know that everything will turn out for the best. It is not saying that all things will be good, but even bad things can work out for our ultimate best. The Lord will not keep us from going through storms, but He promises to be with us, as we do go through them.

THE PROMISE

Holly Boston | Women's Ministry Director

"Trust in the Lord with all your heart, and do not lean on your own understanding. In all your ways acknowledge him, and he will make straight your paths" (Proverbs 3:5,6).

These have come to be my life verses; the first scripture I ever committed to memory. In my experience, they hold the key to experiencing all of God's promises and blessings. God gives us three steps to walking His way that always leads to blessing. First, we must trust in our Heavenly Father, placing our confidence completely in Him. Second, we must lean on Him alone, placing our full weight upon Him. Third, we must completely submit to His authority. Not an easy task when His way often eludes our finite minds.

Consider Abraham; God told him to leave his country, his family, and everything he knew to go to an undetermined place. For those of you who use GPS, this would boggle the mind. For those of us who are planners, the notion of leaving to go 'who knows where' is at best anxiety provoking. Yet Abraham trusted, leaned on, and submitted to God, which ultimately lead to the Promised Land and fulfillment of incredible promises (Genesis 12). Consider Moses; God called him to return to Egypt and persuade Pharaoh to allow the Israelites to leave and worship their God. This must have defied logic considering Moses was a wanted man in Egypt, and he would be required to use his biggest weakness, his tongue, to succeed in the mission. After much questioning and arguing, Moses trusted, leaned on, and submitted to God. This ultimately led to freeing an entire nation.

I was raised in the 70's and 80's, in a home where the things of God were never taught or discussed. I was encouraged to be opinionated, assertive, and dependent on no one: "Be able to support yourself, in case." I was often told that I would make a good attorney due to my "powers of persuasion" and ability to argue. Submission was a four-letter word and not the makings of a good Christian.

In 1995, I received Christ as my Savior and the rough road to transformation began. By 2000, I had three children, and as promised, we were raising them in my husband's church, which was steeped in doctrine, but lacking truth. My desire to attend a Bible teaching church led to heated conversations with my husband and for the first time, my words were not persuasive. Out of desperation, I cried out to God and surrendered my desires and specifically MY ways to Him. Much to my amazement, I knew God wanted me to close my mouth and let Him work. This baffled me. How would my husband ever understand if I do not convince Him? I made a decision to trust, lean on, and submit to my God. Almost immediately, God began to use my children and the clergy of our church to show my husband our need. The final straw was when our education director told my husband, "We don't really know who was created first: Adam or Eve." Within weeks, we were attending Faith Church, seated at the feet of Jesus, and hearing the Word of God.

Over the years, God has been faithful to His promise to show me His path as I have trusted, leaned on, and submitted to Him. The path is not always easy as Abraham and Moses would both attest to. However, I have learned His path always brings blessing.

I have learned God will deliver His people as promised (Psalm 119:170), but in His way (Isaiah 55:9) and in His time (Ecclesiastes 3:1). He will provide "according to His riches" (Philippians 4:19) and "richly bless all who call on Him" (Romans 10:12).

Today, my husband and three children have been saved by the blood of Christ and have declared their faith through Biblical baptism. God has done far more than I ever imagined. (Ephesians 3:20). He made it all possible through a powerful six-letter word: submit!

PAPER SHREDDER

Dr. Randy Johnson | Growth Pastor

It has been a blessing to hear of some of God's promises to us this week. One of the promises that has always awed me is His willingness to forgive us.

1 John 1:9 says, *"If we confess our sins, he is faithful and just to forgive us our sins and to cleanse us from all unrighteousness."* He will cleanse us.

In His later days in referring to His death, Jesus says, *"For this is my blood of the covenant, which is poured out for many for the forgiveness of sins"* (Matthew 26:28).

Psalm 103:12 says, *"As far as the east is from the west, so far does he remove our transgressions from us."* God speaks in extremes in trying to convey the magnitude of His forgiveness.

Micah 7:19 brings up a couple of aspects of the Lord's forgiveness, *"He will again have compassion on us; he will tread our iniquities underfoot. You will cast all our sins into the depths of the sea."* He is having compassion on us while stomping on our sin. He loves the sinner, not the sin. He even casts our sin into the deep waters. We need to remind ourselves that this is a no fishing zone. God has forgiven us, and we need to accept it, forgive ourselves, and press forward.

Isaiah 43:25 says, *"I, I am he who blots out your transgressions for my own sake, and I will not remember your sins."* He blots out our sin. It cannot be seen.

Ephesians 1:7 adds, *"In him we have redemption through his blood, the forgiveness of our trespasses, according to the riches of his grace."* We are forgiven in Jesus.

Hebrews 10:17 says, *"I will remember their sins and their lawless deeds no more."* God chooses to forget our sins. I view it as a paper shredder. My sin is like an IOU that has been placed in a shredder. It no longer can be used against me.

2 Corinthians 5:17 reminds us, *"Therefore, if anyone is in Christ, he is a new creation. The old has passed away; behold, the new has come."* We have a fresh start.

We need to heed the advice that Jesus gave the woman in John 8. He forgives her but instructs her to *"go and sin no more."* I agree with the bumper sticker that says, "Christians aren't perfect, only forgiven." However, that should not give us an excuse. We need to gratefully accept God's forgiveness, forgive others, and strive to be holy because He is holy.

2

God's Plan

John Sanchez | Deacon of Finances

Don't you love a great plan? One that is well thought out, designed perfectly, and flawless in execution? Some of my favorite movie scenes are ones that involve finely honed strategies that are executed with speed and precision. Perhaps we are drawn to those things we find so elusive in real-life. As we know, our plans never play out exactly as we intend for them to. Often, they miss the mark entirely. One of my favorite quotes is "The best-laid plans of mice and men, often go awry." A poet penned it over 200 years ago. It is recognized the world-over today because it rings too true.

God's plans, however, are another thing entirely. His plan for mankind is written throughout history. His plan extends from the beginning of time, pointing us to the coming Messiah, and through to the present day looking for His return. God's plans are fascinating in our understanding and mysterious in their complexity. Only an all-knowing, all-powerful, all-present Heavenly Father can weave the course of human events into the tapestry of His foretold plan of salvation for the entire world.

We will look at what the foretelling of the Messiah may have meant to the people who were part of Jesus lineage, which are the folks who walked the earth before His revelation or birth. Christ's birth is usually something we look at in the past, understandably so. However, for a few moments, during this lesson, let's pretend to look through the eyes of those who did not share the benefit we have of hindsight. For them, the story of the Messiah's birth was a speculative discussion of "who, what, when, and where" - as understood from the writing of the various prophets.

The 'Family Tree'

Do you have a family tree? Actually, we all do. What I mean is, have you ever mapped out your ancestry on paper? Have you outlined the broad, rich history of the many people that make up your lineage? In Matthew chapter 1, we find Jesus' family tree.

Take a minute and read Matthew 1:1-17. Do any names seem familiar to you? Are there any names in Jesus' family tree that surprise you? _____
_____
_____

Can you pick out the following in Jesus' family tree?
A prostitute? _____
An adulteress? _____
A non-Jew? _____
A murderer? _____

What thoughts come to mind as you ponder this list of Jesus' heritage? What do you suppose this says about God, and His plan for mankind? _____
_____
_____
_____
_____

Reading through Jesus' lineage brings to mind a funny TV show my wife and I once watched. The star of the show went on an enthusiastic pursuit to map out his family tree. He was certain that there was royalty in his lineage. By the end of the show, his exercise went tragically wrong when he discovered he was a distant descendant of Adolf Hitler, which he neurotically labored throughout the rest.

Salmon, father of Boaz

Not much is known about Salmon who lived some 1400 years before Christ. During this time in Bible history, there were not many recorded Messianic prophecies. Those prophets mainly appear around 700 BC. Salmon grew up learning of the history of his people's arrival in Egypt under Joseph's 'Messianic' saving of their people from starvation (Genesis 37) and years later as slaves in Egypt, being freed from bondage by God under the leading of the messianic figure of their time – Moses.

During this era of the Bible, we see 'pictures' of Christ woven into recorded history. Imagine for a moment that you were Salmon's schoolmate listening to the stories of their ancestors' slavery in Egypt. Hearing how God preserved Moses' life and his rise to lead the Jewish people out of Egypt.

Stories of true-life accounts can leave fixed impressions in people's minds. Since young minds are very impressionable, there can be little doubt that young Salmon was in many ways affected by this account of his people's history, especially of his people's regard for this leader called Moses.

Recalling the stories of Joseph (Genesis 37) and Moses (Exodus 1), what Christ-like characteristics do we see in these major figures in biblical history? _____

_____

_____

What kind of thoughts or struggles would a young man with a family history like Salmon be guarded or insecure about? How could those issues feed into his sense of awareness of a need for God in his life? _____

_____

_____

Most of us can identify with how our direct life experiences affect our personalities and outlook, but how can our family history affect us the same way? People sometimes find themselves trying to hide or escape ugly truths of their family history. While others seem to shrink in fear from feeling the overwhelming need to live up to the expectations of others – in the shadow of a prominent family member. How do you think Salmon's family history pushes him to a need that can only be filled by God? _____

_____

_____

_____

Josiah, son of Amos

Josiah is one of my favorite kings of Israel. Though not much is spoken of him today, he was eight years old when he became king. We find his story in 2 Kings 22-23. Horrified by the revelation of Israel's unfaithfulness to God's, he set himself on a crusade to destroy idolatry from the land and executed all the pagan priests. Not satisfied with stopping there, he also ordered the bones of the dead false teachers to be exhumed and burned on the altar until there was literally no trace left of them on earth. That is not bad for the young king.

For all his zealous pursuit to save his nation from pending doom, God's promise was merely to delay His judgment until after Josiah's days have passed.

How do you suppose the thought of imminent judgment on his country affected Josiah? _____
_____
_____

How do you think you would respond in his shoes, knowing nothing can be done to erase God's judgment on sin?
_____
_____
_____

How could this awareness awaken in Josiah a burning desire for mercy and forgiveness? _____
_____
_____

It is during this era that Josiah could have been knowledgeable of prophetic words regarding the coming Messiah of Israel.
"For the LORD is our judge; the LORD is our lawgiver; the LORD is our king; he will save us" (Isaiah 33:22).

How meaningful do you think this prophecy would have been to young King Josiah? How does this speak to his specific struggles, hopes, and dreams?
_____
_____

Consider these prophecies Josiah may have been studied in:

"But you, O Bethlehem Ephrathah, who are too little to be among the clans of Judah, from you shall come forth for me one who is to be ruler in Israel, whose coming forth is from of old, from ancient days" (Micah 5:2).

"When Israel was a child, I loved him, and out of Egypt I called my son" (Hosea 11:1).

What do these prophecies indicate where the Messiah will come from? Could this be confusing to Josiah? Would it be confusing to anyone living in these times? _____

_____

_____

God's plan is perfect, never flawed. The truth is, the prophecies above were both true. As we now know (having the benefit of history behind us instead of before us), Jesus was born in Bethlehem (Matthew 2:1-6). When Herod sought to have him killed, Joseph and Mary exiled for a brief time to Egypt. After Herod's death, God spoke to Joseph to return to his home in safety (Matthew 2:14-15). This is another example of God's plan woven through the course of human events.

Do you ever wonder why events occur in your life that does not make sense? Could Josiah have experienced these same feelings and questions when he walked this earth? God's plan does not always make sense to us. Sometimes, as we see in the Bible, His plans are much bigger than our perspective. Our part, though small in the grand heavenly scheme things, is still integral to the tapestry of His plan.

Joseph and Mary

Most of us need no introduction to Joseph and Mary. When it comes to the story of Jesus' birth, they share the stage with the star of the show.

Have we ever considered how this 'Good News' of the Messiah's birth looked like from their perspective? Few would argue them to be blessed in all the earth to have such a privilege. Their son Jesus held the hopes and dreams of all of Israel. Yet, His introduction to the world affected their lives in profound ways.

"Therefore the Lord himself will give you a sign. Behold, a virgin shall conceive and bear a son, and shall call his name Immanuel" (Isaiah 7:14).

No doubt, generations had learned about the prophecies spoken by Isaiah, most notably this one in particular. You can almost imagine the many people reading in awe and wonder of such a miraculous sign. "How could that be?" some may have asked themselves. Only God could do such a thing. Here is Mary, living out the fulfillment of this marvelous prophetic word.

However, what are the consequences of being chosen by God to partake in the marvelous unfolding of His plan? Did the nation of Israel celebrate her good news? Was her state honored and supported by everyone around her? Would you consider her situation 'comfortable'? _____

_____

_____

_____

Have you ever found yourself in an undesirable situation that was not of your choice or making? How did it make you feel? How did it affect you and those around you as well? _____

_____

_____

_____

Mary, blessed among all women, was entrusted by God to be a part of His plan. He saw in her a godly humility and servant's heart He could trust. It was a great honor that carried great responsibility.

Likewise, Joseph was a just man. Scripture tells us in Matthew 1:19 that his inclination was to show grace and mercy to Mary before God's plan was revealed to him.

How do you think Joseph's life was affected by his decision to proceed in marriage with Mary? What do you suppose this meant to his reputation among his family, friends, and countrymen? How could this have affected his life? In what ways?

_____

_____

_____

_____

Joseph, coming alongside Mary, was entrusted by God to be a part of His plan. Who among the people of Israel would not have wanted to be so honored? However, living it out looks quite different. It is not too hard to see the weight of the 'call' certainly takes the glamor out of the situation very fast. Joseph and Mary, looking for the Messiah through the eyes of the Prophets, became part of the prophetic foretelling. In so doing, they became the supporting cast to the greatest Plan to ever unfold in history.

God's Word is so much more than historical accounts. It is the living and breathing Word of God that was written for us. *"For whatever was written in former days was written for our instruction, that through endurance and through the encouragement of the Scriptures we might have hope"* (Romans 15:4).

God's plan did not end with the last chapter of the Bible. It is still alive and well today.

What is God's plan for you? For your family? For your world?

_____

_____

_____

_____

_____

Perhaps that question conjures up fantastic ideas in our minds, but as God's Word reveals to us, what it actually looks and feels like may be the furthest from our imagination. Perhaps your toils, struggles, or the 'mundane-ness' of life may be God working in your life. His plans are usually at work despite what we think or see.

STAND APART

Roger Allen | Facilities Director

A merica is the land of self-improvement. Whether it be home, spiritual, physical, or financial. TV land is filled with the latest and greatest fixes. Doctors provide us a cure for our insecurities. Drug companies promise us nirvana. Invest in this and you will be rich. Eat this and you will be thin. The list goes on and on. This is not only true for unbelievers; it is how we as believers live our lives.

While there can be some benefit in self–improvement, let's not mistake it for God's plan for our life. Through His Word, we have been given the perfect instruction for our life. The plan is not the latest and greatest fix in our everyday life. It is to surrender and follow Him daily with our whole heart. Our personal successes and selfish desires do not equate God's Plan for us.

Nothing pleases God more than letting Him change and refine us. Through obedience, prayer, and surrendering to Him, He allows us to have an active role in the process as He molds us for His glory. We are called to be set apart, not conforming to the world's standard. It is the desire of God for believers to be sanctified. For many, sanctification brings uneasiness. We know that we are not worthy or capable of achieving it on our own. It is only through the cross and the shed blood of Jesus Christ that we are sanctified. Hebrews 13:12 says, ***"So Jesus also suffered outside the gate in order to sanctify the people through his own blood."***

As sons and daughters of the Most High, we have the Holy Spirit that dwells within us to convict, inspire, and lead us into a relationship with Him. As we go about planning our life and searching for the next "fix," let us not forget that God desires a relationship with us. The Creator of the universe wants to enjoy our presence and fellowship with us. In His limitless grace, that is God's plan for each one of us.

"I appeal to you therefore, brothers, by the mercies of God, to present your bodies as a living sacrifice, holy and acceptable to God, which is your spiritual worship. Do not be conformed to this world] but be transformed by the renewal of your mind, that by testing you may discern what is the will of God, what is good and acceptable and perfect" (Romans 12:1-2).

ANSWER THE CALL

Roger Allen | Facilities Director

> **"*And I heard the voice of the Lord saying, 'Whom shall I send, and who will go for us?' Then I said, 'Here I am! Send me'"* (Isaiah 6:8).**

What if God asked you to quit your job to help the homeless or sell all of your possessions and move away, would you? Would your faith allow you to pack and leave all you know at God's calling? Would fear overcome you when it is time to move? Would we base our decision on faith and faith alone? The closer we pull toward God the more legitimate this becomes. Our actions become more intentional, and our thoughts are more defined. As God directs our path, we become more pliable and more willing to accept His plan for our lives. What we thought was impossible is now more real than ever. He is calling. Will we answer?

The Bible is filled with those who answered the call, from Abraham to the disciples. Through faith, prayer, the Holy Spirit, and the Word, they were able to determine His call. God equipped them for the journey. Faith, words, strength, and stamina were given when needed. He used the simple to confound the wise. His plan fulfilled.

To reach out to others with the "Good News" is ultimately what He asks. His plan will proceed with or without us. The cost is small compared to the reward. Will we let fear keep us from achieving what He has for us? Will the seed of doubt grow and prevent us from the prosperous life God had intended? Or, will we boldly say 'send me' when He calls? Going forward with the promise that it is better in the will of God, than the alternative would be. We will proclaim His glory to all!

"For God gave us not a spirit of fearfulness; but if power and love and discipline" (2 Timothy 1:7).

GOD'S WILL

Dave Zidel

How has God revealed His will and plan to you in the most unexpected way?

Have you ever thought about how amazing God is and that He is not bound by time, space, or matter. God is far off and near at the same time, in the past, present, and future. In Him, we move, live, and have our being. Have you ever thought about what His will and plans are for your life and the opportunities you have to encourage others?

In November 2014, I was let go from my job. I was able to save my home with a HARP loan, but I was still trying to get back on my feet financially. Being unemployed was difficult enough, but now I had other financial responsibilities.

About a month later, someone ran a stop sign and damaged my car. I immediately began to ask, "Why more problems Lord?" Financially speaking, it was more than I wanted to bear, but I was trusting God and knew that He had a plan. I focused on Jeremiah 29:11: *"For I know the plans I have for you, declares the Lord, plans for welfare and not for evil, to give you a future and a hope."*

I remembered the problems that Joseph went through. As you may remember, Joseph's brothers sold him into slavery. Genesis 39:2 says, *"The Lord was with Joseph."* Instead of getting angry because of his circumstances, Joseph trusted God. Later, he was falsely accused by Potiphar's wife and was thrown into prison. Again the Bible says in Genesis 39:21 that the *"The Lord was with Joseph"* and showed him mercy.

I am sure Joseph was wondering what God's plan was for him being sold into slavery, or being put into prison. However, isn't it encouraging knowing that God never forsook Joseph? In fact, God used this experience to prepare him for an even greater position in the Egyptian kingdom. How about you? Can you think of a time when you had hardships that worked out for God's purpose? Have you shared this with those going through hard times?

About a week after the accident, Michigan's mini-tort provided me with $1,000 that helped pay the bills. While I was unemployed, I had the opportunity to volunteer in the construction at our church, where later I was hired to work. God works in mysterious ways. In your darkest hour, how has God been with you and shown you His plans for you?

GOD'S TIMING VS. OUR TIMING

Bryan Fox | Deacon of Facilities

"He said to them 'It is not for you to know the times or dates the Father has set by His own authority'" (Acts 1:7).

Every good and loving relationship requires a degree of patience. A close relationship with God means that your patience will be rewarded. It may not fit your schedule but it will come exactly when it is supposed to according to God's schedule.

Looking back at my life, I can see where I had made plans for my life that did not come close to happening. Before I had a relationship with Jesus, my plans were all about the world. Climbing the corporate ladder, making money, and being a success were my plans. While I accomplished a lot, I still felt a void. I missed too much family life, people who I thought were my friends would vanish, and I realized that my bosses were after only one thing... their success, not mine.

After I accepted Jesus as my Savior, my plans (which included doing more for the church) still did not happen according to my plans and timetable.

Ecclesiastes 3:11 says, *"He has made everything beautiful in its time He has also set eternity in the human heart; yet no one can fathom what God has done from beginning to end."*

God knows my life from beginning to end. I find that when I allow my plans and pride to dictate how I live my life, I will be humbled and awed when God reveals His plan for me.

I am not saying that you cannot or should not have plans and goals for the day, week, or year, but you need to have a deep and loving relationship with God and beg for wisdom asking Him to reveal His plans to you. Then you can look around in your daily life and see more easily what you should be doing to please Him.

Proverbs 3:5–6 says, *"Trust in the Lord with all your heart, and do not lean on your own understanding. In all your ways acknowledge Him and He will make straight your paths."*

Isaiah 55:8–9 adds, *"For my thoughts are not your thoughts, neither are your ways my ways, declares the Lord. For as the heavens are higher than the earth, so are my ways higher than your ways and my thoughts than your thoughts."*

CONTROL LIMITS GOD'S PLAN

Bryan Fox | Deacon of Facilities

P arents will ask their children "what do you want to be when you grow up?" Although this may not be a bad question to get children to realize that at some point they will need to do something to make a living and to provide for their future family, children really do not have a clue as to what they will do in life. Kids go into high school and then college with plans of wanting this or that for a career, but how many change their degree in midstream or finish college and enter into a field that they did not specialize in?

The real question should be what does God want me to be and do in life?

Jeremiah 29:11: *"For I know the plans I have for you, declares the LORD, plans for welfare and not for evil, to give you a future and a hope."*

I look at my life from the perspective of it being over half over and see when I lived according to my plans I was able to provide for my family, however, something was missing.

It was not until I accepted Jesus as my Lord and Savior that I started looking at life differently. I went from attending church on special occasions only to attending on a regular basis. Then I even started getting involved with "church people" and actually wanting to learn The Word. I began to pray for God's will to be revealed to me. Over time, His will was revealed, and I was given the opportunity to work in ministry serving the people that I have come to know and love.

Proverbs 16:3 says, *"Commit your work to the Lord, and your plans will be established."*

It is truly a blessing to know that you are being used where God wants you to be. Sometimes I wish that I had come around a lot sooner in life, but I cannot live in the past.

I urge you to ask God for wisdom and for Him to reveal His will for you and your life. No matter where you are now though, look for opportunities to show Jesus to those around you and share the Gospel. Please do not miss an opportunity that God has given you to share the Good News of Jesus.

LOVE TIMES LOVE
EQUALS ACCOMPLISHED

William Kinney | Facilities

*"**F**or we are his workmanship, created in Christ Jesus for good works, which God prepared beforehand, that we should walk in them"* (Ephesians 2:10).

We are all made by design and beautiful. He crafted us with love and care. We are all made in His image to do His will, regardless if your tall or short, big or small, smart or not, strong or weak, male or female. He made us just the way He intended us to be. We need to embrace and love who we are because we are all made in His image - to love Him.

We as believers have to surrender our life to our Heavenly Father and love Him with all our hearts. That is the reason He made us - so we can love Him and be His friend, family, and servant. As believers, we have to be the door where His love can come into the world. Therefore, to love God, we have to love all people.

In Matthew 22:36-40 we read:

"'Teacher, which is the great commandment in the Law?' And he said to him, 'You shall love the Lord your God with all your heart and with all your soul and with all your mind. This is the great and first commandment. And a second is like it: You shall love your neighbor as yourself. On these two commandments depend all the Law and the Prophets.'"

We as followers of Christ think we need to find His plan for our life. However, His plan is simple - Love Him with all our hearts and soul. We have to be tireless servants to Him and reflectors of

His love to our neighbors. Each of us can show that love to others in our own uniquely talented ways.

We as believers must not sit on the sidelines. We are called to serve any way we can. There is always a way to show others God's love no matter where you live, work, or play.

Where we are is where we are called to be. That is your mission field.

3

God's Purpose

Pastor Chuck Lindsey | Reach Pastor

"**D**ad! Hurry! Come quick!" came the rather loud shout from my 12-year-old son. As I ran to the backyard to make sure he was not hurt, I saw him standing in front of a large mound of dirt with his arm outstretched, finger pointing, and his mouth open. As I looked closer, I saw what appeared to be a city, a million strong, of red fire ants weaving their way in and out of that mound of dirt.

What I did next surprised my son. I immediately shouted, "Dear ants! I love each and every one of you with an everlasting love!" Then, I got down on my knees and began to try to hug that mound of dirt determined to show my affection for them! Ok, the last part, I completely made up!

However, what if it were true? What a strange thing right? Some of you would immediately skip this chapter of the book concluding that I had lost my mind and needed professional help! You would be right! However, indulge me with this story for a minute.

What if you DID, IN FACT, LOVE ants? What if they WERE all you thought about? What if, (as love always does) you wanted to communicate your love for them in some real way? How could you do that? Would you gather them up and talk to them? Would you try to hold them in your hands or bring them close to hug them? Would you invite them into your home to live with you? Would you buy them gifts at Christmas? (What does one buy an ant for Christmas?)

These are silly examples of course but think about it...

How would you effectively communicate your love to them?

_____

_____

_____

How would you convey your desire to have a relationship with them? _____

_____

_____

There is only one answer. You would have to become one of them. Once you did, then every possible "ant" way of communication and expression would be possible and open to you. In short, you would speak their language.

Two thousand years ago, a baby was born to a poor couple who wrapped Him in strips of cloth and laid Him in the feeding trough of a small barn. That baby was God Himself wrapped in human flesh! John 1:1 tells us that *"in the beginning was the Word and the Word was with God and the Word WAS GOD"* and verse 14 tells us, *"and the WORD became flesh and DWELT AMONG US."* Now listen, He was a real baby (not some "super human being" pretending to be a baby!) with real crying, real dirty diapers, and a continual need to eat (and all the moms said? "Amen!")

When did Jesus begin? _____
_____
_____

Who is the Word in John chapter 1? _____
_____
_____
_____

He was born. Think of that. He did not just appear. He was born! For the first time in all of eternity, He was helpless, dependent, weak, and needing. He grew. He was a two-year-old. He was a five-year-old. He was a seven-year-old. He was a 12 year old. He was even a teenager! He went through puberty, His voice changed and cracked. He worked and became tired. He was hungry and thirsty and got sick like you do in the winter months. He had friends, family, and went to people's homes for dinner. When He hit his thumb with His hammer He probably shouted "Hallelujah!"

What part of Jesus being human is awkward for you to think about? _____
_____
_____

What part of Jesus being human is most comforting to you?
_____
_____
_____
_____

This baby, this God man, came not by accident or by chance but rather as a fulfillment of an eternal plan. A plan to rescue us, those He loves, to save us from our sins, and to unite us to Himself forever! In short, He came to "speak our language" and tell us He has always loved us with an everlasting love. He would do all of that on a single day on a wooden cross.

What was God's plan in having Jesus come to earth?

_____

_____

_____

Throughout the Gospels, we see that our Jesus had the purpose of His coming ALWAYS in mind. His whole life, sort of, crescendos to what He called "the hour" of His coming. That "hour" He said would come. At 33 years of age, that hour finally came. In that "hour" He would allow the people He had created, the very ones He was trying to tell... to take Him, beat Him, mock Him, scourge Him, and hang Him on a wooden cross. This was His purpose, His mission, and the reason He had come. He was born to die. He did die that day (spoiler alert! He rose three days later). As the source of all life and light hung there, the Father shrouded the world in total darkness. It is there that Jesus paid for our sins and definitively said, "Here is the proof of my love for you!" Jesus Himself said in John 15, *"no greater example of love can be shown, that for one to lay down his life for the one he loves."* Our Jesus did that. Therefore, we say with Paul in Galatians that He truly *"loved us and gave Himself for us."* For *"The Son of Man has come to seek and to save that which was lost."*

So, think back, to those ants at the beginning of our story and consider that our God came to us, born as one of us, grew up among us, died for us, and then was risen from the dead for us, all so that we would know Him and how deeply He loves us. He gave His life for us, may we daily give back to Him the only "gift" He has ever wanted... us.

What does it mean to give ourselves to God? _____

_____

_____

Is it just a one-time thing or can it also be daily? _____

_____

_____

What area do you still need to give to God (or give Him again)?

_____

_____

_____

PLAN AND PURPOSE

Debbie Gabbara | Community Center Director

"*I* *make known the end from the beginning, from ancient times, what is still to come. I say, 'My purpose will stand, and I will do all that I please'*" (Isaiah 46:10 NIV).

God has always had a plan, and you were always on His mind. His purpose was always to have a relationship with you.

What a wonderful time of year this is! All around us, people are getting ready for Christmas. Whether or not they talk about it, the fact is, this holiday is to celebrate the birth of Jesus. The birth of the one who, from the beginning of time, knew His purpose was to be born in a manger and to die on a cross to save all mankind.

Many circumstances would prove unable to stop the plans of God. Mary, a young unwed girl, learns that she is going to have a baby. Who would ever believe that she had been visited by an angel and told that she would be the mother of God's Son? She could have been stoned, but she was not.

A fearful king ordered to have all the boys in the area under two years old killed because he was afraid of one baby he had heard talk of, one who was called King of the Jews. Jesus should have been among those children, but God had told Joseph to take Jesus and Mary and flee to Egypt. About thirty years later, it looked like God's plan had failed when Jesus died on a cross. However, this too was part of the Father's plan. Without a perfect sacrifice to cover our sins, we could never have the relationship God has always wanted to have with us. Jesus always knew His purpose; He came to die so that we might have eternal life.

God's purpose may not always look like it makes sense from the point of view from where we stand. However, the Bible says God's ways are not our ways. Things are not always as they seem. Three days after His death, Jesus would arise to life. Remember, God said, "My purpose will stand, and I will do all that I please."

We serve a risen Savior! Tell everyone you know this Christmas. We celebrate the birth of Jesus. His plan was always that you and I might learn of Him, believe in Him, choose Him, tell of our love for Him, and help others to understand that God's plan is for them!

"For unto us a child is born, to us a son is given, and the government will be on his shoulders. And he will be called Wonderful, Counselor, Mighty God, Everlasting Father, Prince of Peace" (Isaiah 9:6 NIV).

"For God so loved the world that he gave his one and only Son, that whoever believes in him shall not perish but have eternal life" (John 3:16 NIV).

WHAT IS YOUR PURPOSE?

Debbie Gabbara | Community Center Director

Do you ever wonder if God has something specifically for you to do? Before you answer, look at this verse. *"For it is God who works in you to will and to act in order to fulfill his good purpose"* (Philippians 2:13 NIV).

Not only does God have things for each of us to do, but God also says He will work in us and will use us to fulfill this good purpose. God has a plan for every one of us! Maybe you are a dentist, maybe a teacher, or stay at home mom. Your place in God's plan may be bagging groceries or doing surgery, working in a fast food restaurant, or clearing snow. Wherever it is, you are in a place where God can use you! Right now, right where you are, God has work planned for us each to do, and He gives us the desire to complete it.

My husband and I recently watched a movie about a man who discovered that finding his purpose was more than just succeeding in life. He was taken on a journey that taught him that finding purpose required:

Seeing – Giving attention to people and things that were going around him.

Feeling – Taking time to evaluate actions, emotions, and circumstances that were affecting his life.

Trusting – Trusting in a God who knows our beginning and our end. A God, who always loves us, and has plans for our lives that are good,

"For I know the plans I have for you," declares the LORD, "plans to prosper you and not to harm you, plans to find you hope and a future. Then you will call on me and come and pray to me, and I will listen to you. You will seek me and find me when you seek me with all your heart. I will be found by you," declares the LORD" (Jeremiah 29:11-13).

All through the Bible God has used people to complete His work. Some of those people sought Him and walked in His ways, and some had no idea that they were a part of God's plan.

Sometimes God's plans are crystal clear to us, more often they are not. When you are uncertain about God's direction for your life, call on Him. Do not give up, seek Him with your whole heart, and pray earnestly. When you do, in His timing, God will answer your prayers and make His plans known to you. The Lord will lead you and give you a heart to know His ways and His plans. You will seek Him and find Him, and you will be eternally grateful that you did.

FINDING PURPOSE

Pat MacDermaid | Clothing Closet

"*And we know that for those who love God all things work together for good, for those who are called according to his purpose*" (Romans 8:28).

This verse tells us without a doubt that God has a plan for all of His children that He knows best. Trust Him to work His perfect purpose out for you.

If we want to know our purpose in God's plan, we need to have a personal Father-child relationship with Him. Think about it. Do you want your children only to come to you for the things they can get from you? I do not think so; we want them to come to us with their hurts, struggles, questions, joys, blessings, big, and small things. We want to be on the inside of their lives. Our Father, the creator of us all, should not get the leftovers of our time, a few crumbs of our day, and maybe a few more as we end the day. I think our Father who called us, saved us, and will one day take us to Heaven wants more than that from us.

If you take quiet time with Him, talk to Him about your day, tell Him everything, you will find He will direct your path. I know that He has mine. If you are willing to let Him use you, trust that He knows what He is doing. You will find yourself running to Him with everything, from the smallest things to the life-changing things. If you are willing to go with Him, He will take you on an adventure and along the way, He will teach you about patience, perseverance, commitment, service, compassion, love, and a whole lot more. You were made for a purpose, one that was made just for you.

I remember a time in my life when I knew God had a purpose for me. I was 42 years old and a widow. I was visiting my mother at her apartment. We were just chatting about nothing in particular. She had gone into the kitchen for more coffee. I could see her from where I was sitting. She looked at me and said, "I tried to get rid of you, but it didn't work. It worked out okay though because your dad loved you." That is not what you want to hear from your mom. That hurt! For weeks, I kept asking God why she did not just keep it to herself. One day I was at a stop light, I asked God again, and this time, I felt that feeling when you get an answer and you know it is from God. He said, "I wanted you to know I wanted you." I knew then that He had things for me to do. When God says He has a purpose for each of us, He means it. I am 71 now, and I know God had a plan for me, or I never would have been born.

Has God ever made something very clear that He wanted you to do?

Did you do it?

Why or why not?

DO YOU NEED
TO BE SLAPPED?

Isaiah Combs | Worship Leader & Young Adults Director

I do not know about you, but knowing God's purpose for your life can be difficult.

I was talking with a friend the other day, and he said, "God usually has to slap me in the face to get my attention." There may have never been a truer statement spoken. We usually have to be slapped in the face by God to see His purpose for us.

We pretend to be actively seeking His purpose. Then when God shows us something, we brush it off as if it was not God giving us an answer. There is an awesome story in Judges about a man named Gideon. Gideon doubted God's purpose for his life at every turn. God sent an Angel to Gideon, and he doubted that it actually was an Angel until he did something amazing to make Gideon believe. Gideon again doubted that God wanted to use him to save the Israelites. He set a piece of fleece outside and asked God to make the fleece wet and the ground dry. God did it. Then Gideon still was not convinced. He asked God to do the opposite; make the fleece dry and the ground wet. God did it. You would think that Gideon would have caught on by then. I like to think that I would have caught on, but probably not.

God ends up using Gideon to defeat the Midianite Army of 125,000 men with 300 men. Though Gideon continued to doubt God and the purpose God had for him. God still used Gideon in a great way. We are a lot like Gideon. We doubt and ask for more and more signs from God.

I knew God wanted me to get out of the military and serve Him full-time. However, I doubted and made up excuses. God made my path out of the military perfect. Every question and worry my wife and I had about the transition was answered, and God protected us the whole way.

Romans 8:28 says, *"For we know that all things work together for good for those that know and love God and are called according to his purpose."*

God has a purpose for your life, and it will work out. It is about time we quit questioning God and let him use us for a His purpose.

PURPOSE TO PROCLAIM HIS POWER

Wes McCullough | Worship Leader

God has a purpose. He has a plan. God's children know that statement with absolute certainty. God is always in control with His perfect plan to glorify Himself and bless His children. However, sometimes we find it nearly impossible to see past our hardships and trust that God will one day turn those struggles into blessings.

Patience and perseverance are not gifts as much as they are learned disciplines. In some cases, waiting on God's purpose to be unveiled to us requires years of suffering and turmoil. This was the case with the Israelites in Egypt who were enslaved for generations. Even after God brought them out of slavery, it took forty years of wandering in the desert to learn to trust in God.

Sometimes God's plan is that you endure years of illness, pain, and discomfort. It can seem endless. You may question why God would put you through all that when you are a faithful, God-fearing believer. I believe the trials God allows us to go through are to prepare us for His future plans. What you experience today as suffering is God teaching you qualities and disciplines you will need later in life as God continues to use you for His glory. *"I have raised you up for this very purpose, that I might show you my power and that my name might be proclaimed in all the earth"* (Exodus 9:16).

You may understand God's plan early in the process. For many people, God's purpose is not revealed until you have weathered the storm and can look back and see the path that at the time seemed hidden but is now obvious. Romans 8:28 says, *"We know that in all things God works for the good of those who*

71

love him, who have been called according to his purpose."
Remain encouraged that in your hard times God has not forgotten about you.

Above all, do not fight God's purpose. Such efforts are wasted. Instead, focus on growing your faith, perseverance, and commitment to God. Though the struggles seem endless, remember that God's purpose is good, you can do all things through Christ, and that His blessings are coming pressed down, shaken together and running over to those who trust in Him.

TO _____ BE THE GLORY

Noble Baird | Guest Services Director

***

P urpose: The reason why something is done or used; the aim or goal of a person; what a person is trying to do, become, etc.

I think if we are honest with each other and ourselves, purpose is something we have struggled with or are struggling with right now. Whatever side of the spectrum you may land on, you are not alone. Searching for God's purpose in our lives takes time, dedication, prayer, and thanking Him for every circumstance He places in our path.

In Judges 3:12-30, we are introduced to Israel's next judge Ehud. At this time, Israel is a mess. They are continually going through these cycles of finding God and following after Him, then sinning and falling away, one of their enemies then captures them and oppressed; finally, they call out to God, and He sends them a redeemer. In this passage, Israel's oppressors are the Moabites and their redeemer comes from the tribe of Benjamin (which none of the Israelites ever expected, since this was the smallest and weakest of the 12 tribes).

As Israel finds themselves being oppressed by the Moabites, they cannot take it anymore and cry out to God. God then calls the man Ehud, to fulfill His purpose in redeeming His people from Moab. However, what many people do not know about Ehud is that he is a left-handed warrior. The reason why this is so is that he physically could not use his right arm since it was deformed. God still used Ehud to kill the king of Moab and restore His people.

The reason I love this story so much is that I can see myself in Ehud. I am not the smartest, strongest, or best looking. I am not a first round pick by any means...yet God still called me and chose to use me in full-time ministry. You see, when we read through the book of Judges God did not call the equipped; He equips those He calls. Why? Why does He equip those He calls and not just simply use those who are already equipped? In Psalm 115:1 David writes, *"Not to us, O LORD, not to us, but to your name give glory, for the sake of your steadfast love and your faithfulness!"* God's purpose for our lives is not that we be glorified, but that He be glorified through us. As you go throughout the rest of this week and month, I challenge you to take a step back and evaluate. Whose purpose are you chasing after, and whom are you glorifying? Yourself and this world, or are you chasing after His purpose for your life and glorifying Him?

4

God's Present

Pastor Ryan Story | Student Pastor

W hile the Christmas season is amazing, it sure can be exhausting. Think about all the time you put into decorating your home, putting up a tree, fighting the crowds to find that perfect gift, baking cookies and other treats, and all the other craziness that goes on during December. Let's be honest about one thing; we love all the holiday chaos. Malls are crazy, but seeing the face of a loved one when they receive their gift makes it worth it. Watching the wonderment in small children as they see all the decorations going up throughout the house makes dealing with tangled lights for hours minor. We are creating memories for a lifetime.

What are some of your favorite Christmas memories?

_____
_____
_____
_____

Do you have any Christmas traditions? _____
_____
_____
_____

While all the hustle and bustle of the holidays is not bad, it can be if we forget that Christmas is the day we celebrate that *"For unto you is born this day in the city of David a Savior, who is Christ the Lord."* This is the moment that changed EVERYTHING. I am sure as a child you asked Santa for some amazing gifts but imagine getting God for Christmas. Mary and Joseph knew their Son was going to be something special. The angel and the heavenly hosts that appeared to the shepherds were so exuberant with their praise they became visible. The wise men traveled for close to three years to visit the Savior of the world. The reason why all these things happened is rooted in one word "Immanuel."

Matthew 1:22-23

"All this took place to fulfill what the Lord had spoken by the prophet: 'Behold, the virgin shall conceive and bear a son, and they shall call his name Immanuel.'"

In your own words, how would you describe why "God with us" is so important? _____

_____

_____

_____

The Old Testament makes up about 75% of the Bible (23,145 Old Testament verses compared to 7,957 New Testament verses). Imagine ripping the pages out the first three-fourths of Moby Dick; we would never know why Ahab was chasing that white whale.

Isaiah 7:10-16

"Again the Lord spoke to Ahaz, 11 'Ask a sign of the Lord your God; let it be deep as Sheol or high as heaven.' 12 But Ahaz said, 'I will not ask, and I will not put the Lord to the test.' 13 And he said, 'Hear then, O house of David! Is it too little for you to weary men, that you weary my God also? 14 Therefore the Lord himself will give you a sign. Behold, the virgin shall conceive and bear a son, and shall call his name Immanuel. 15 He shall eat curds and honey when he knows how to refuse the evil and choose the good. 16 For before the boy knows how to refuse the evil and choose the good, the land whose two kings you dread will be deserted.'"

Why is it vital we know that God was sending "Immanuel" to us?

_____

_____

_____

How is "God with us" different from "us with God"? _____

_____

_____

_____

In Genesis, God created everything and had perfect fellowship with Adam and Eve for a short time. As a result of sin, that fellowship was broken. Fast forward to Jesus being born, and Jesus' work on the cross. Because of His sacrifice we can, once again, regain that "perfect fellowship." One great thing about Christmas is how it brings everyone together. I do not get to spend Christmas with my brother and sister often, but there is nothing sweeter than when I get to.

Revelation 21:3

"And I heard a loud voice from the throne saying, 'Behold, the dwelling place of God is with man. He will dwell with them, and they will be his people, and God himself will be with them as their God.'"

How is this the "ultimate Christmas gift?" _____

_____

_____

_____

The book of Matthew opens with the idea of "God with us." It also wraps up with this same idea. It seems as if Matthew wanted us to know that one of the central purposes of Jesus is that He is with us.

Matthew 28:19-20

"Go therefore and make disciples of all nations, baptizing them in the name of the Father and of the Son and of the Holy Spirit, 20 teaching them to observe all that I have commanded you. And behold, I am with you always, to the end of the age."

Why is "God with us" so important as we are reaching the lost?

_____

_____

_____

Jesus with us means change is possible.

Merry Christmas!

YOU JUST HAD TO BE THERE

Jared Bruder | Growth Intern

"**Y**ou just had to be there." We all have at least one event in our lives that at times seem impossible to explain to someone who was not there. One such event from my life was the night I got lost. My running companion, Chris, and I went out for what seemed to be a typical night training run. At this time, I was helping Chris train for his first 100-mile endurance run. Every Friday we would hit Island Lake State Park for a 50-kilometer (31 miles) training run. Strapped with headlamps, we would hit the trails about 9 o'clock in the evening. We had run these trails countless times. On the trail, there was a fork and we always stayed to the right of the fork. On this particular night, we decided to take the left. Before we knew what happened we realized that we were no longer running on a trail, and we did not know how to get back to the trail. At 2 am we were lost in a vast State Park after running over 20 miles. In a panic trying to find the trail, we crossed two rivers that were almost neck deep on me. After what seemed like years, we found the trail and finished our run. It is near impossible to explain how we felt being totally lost in the middle of the woods in the middle of the night. You do not understand; you just had to be there.

There is a time in all of our lives where we did not understand what it means to be a follower of Jesus Christ. We did not understand what it meant to see the Spirit move or to see God do a work. It is the concept that you have to be a Jesus follower to understand. I Corinthians 2 addresses this concept in verses 13-14 which say, *"And we impart this in words not taught by human wisdom but taught by the Spirit, interpreting spiritual truths to those who are spiritual. The natural person does not accept the things of the Spirit of God, for they are folly to him, and he is not able to understand them because they are spiritually discerned."* Jesus has given us the gift of understanding. This understanding comes through the Holy Spirit who lives within us.

As a believer, we now have events in our life that start with the phrase, "you just had to be there." I cannot put into words all that God has done for me in my life. Jesus saved my soul from hell, and there is no way I can put into words the joy that is within me. All I can say is I thank God for the gifts He has given through our Lord and Savior Jesus Christ. If you have not accepted Christ into your life, you just will not understand. If you want to understand simply recognize you are a sinner, believe Jesus paid the penalty for your sins, ask Him to save you from your sins, and then you can begin to understand what it means to have Christ in your life.

GOD'S GIFTS & SANTA'S GIFTS

Pastor Ryan Story | Student Pastor

I remember how spectacular Christmas was when I was a child. As a kid making my Christmas list, there was nothing I could not ask for. I asked for any and everything without the first thought about how much those things cost. However, as I got older, my list went from child-filled wonderment to things that were more practical and necessary. I stopped asking for everything and started for more of a realistic choice. Adulthood starts to replace childlike awe, not just about Christmas but also about life. While that was helpful for anyone shopping for me at Christmas, the healthy shift in my wish list reflected an unhealthy shift in my heart.

Now I grew up in a non-Christian household. There was no Jesus during Christmas, but I did lose something, as I grew older. I lost that childlike faith that only small children have. Now I cannot look at my life and recount the times as a child that I believed in Jesus, but I can look back and think about when I started looking at Jesus differently. For the next two days, I wanted to look at the ways children look at Santa and the way we should look at God.

Santa does run out of gifts. God does not run out.

Have you ever seen a Christmas list from a child? Those things are well thought out and long. No matter how crazy of a request, children ask Santa for gifts with no fear of supply or demand. A child never expects to see a note from Santa that reads, "Sorry Tommy, we ran out." As a Christian, have you ever gotten to a place where you do not feel like God can help you? You find yourself thinking that your weekly quota of grace and love has been exceeded so you cannot ask God for forgiveness (Psalm 103:12). Your walk with Jesus has been unstable so you cannot ask Him to *"make straight your path"* (Proverbs 3). Children can look to a man in red and believe that he is unlimited. Those of us who know the one true God, who have *"tasted and seen his goodness"* (Psalm 34) have a tendency of limited God.

It never burdens Santa.

Ask any child about Santa's workload. In every story you read, any movie you watch, he and the elves start working the day after Christmas. The list starts to be made, the toys start to be constructed, and the reindeer need to engage in their games. The whole operation that Santa runs is over the top. Yet no child would ever say that he or she is burdening Santa because the child believes he is capable of doing anything.

Do you believe that God can do anything? Most every Christian would say, yes, but take a moment and think of a time you felt that you were a bother to God. It may just be me, but I have found myself praying for the same thing, pleading for help with the same struggles, and failing daily. I felt like the reason I was not "getting it" was because God was annoyed with me. The reality all the work it takes to make the universe operate like clockwork, all the work needed to allow our circulatory and nervous system to run properly, is not even on God's radar when it comes to a burden. He is almighty; therefore, no amount of work could ever burden our Lord. Take some time to read Psalm 55, God cannot become tired, He cannot become faint, and He is so strong He requests our burdens.

HE NEVER LOOKS DOWN ON US FOR ASKING

Pastor Ryan Story | Student Pastor

I remember asking Santa for some pretty crazy things. I was a huge basketball fan as a kid and for some reason, I thought Charles Barkley was awesome. I remember asking Santa for a 76er's jersey signed by Sir Charles himself. Now clearly in 1989, that would have been a hard thing for "Santa" to get me, but it did not stop me from asking. There was never a moment that I felt like Santa thought I was a fool for asking.

Have you ever needed to ask God for something and you were a bit afraid of it? I have worked with students for some time now, and a lot of times when a teenager wants to pray for a member of their family, they have some thought in their head that God cannot help them. There are times where I have talked with teenagers who are struggling with issues, and they think God will be mad if they confess their sins to Him. Somehow, we believe that the man with a belly like a bowl full of jelly is more understanding than the creator of the universe!

God honors bold faith. One of my favorite Old Testament stories is when Joshua asked God to stop the sun from setting. Feel free to read Joshua 10, but there is never a moment when God says to Joshua, "Hey that is too crazy, leave me alone." Read the Bible, if a person is asking God with a pure heart and the correct motives, He never looks down on us for having the faith to ask Him for the impossible.

No Race or Gender Bias

One day my brother and I were having a heated argument filled with the most intellectual and logical statements a six and seven year old could muster. The argument was over the description on the back of our Teenage Mutant Ninja Turtle's Party Van. I was convinced that Santa only delivered gifts in English, while my brother took the stance that he would have changed the language it was made in. It did not make sense to me why Santa would change the language because clearly, every Santa I ever saw in the mall was white and Anglo Saxon. Why would he treat a random Swedish child with the same love as me? In my head, I was convicted that since I wrote the letters, and I visited Santa in the mall, I was clearly the favorite.

I am glad I have a bit more of a worldview than I had when I was six. As a kid, I figured Santa favored Americans. I feel that as Christians we sometimes take that worldview. Imagine having the worldview that Jesus is for the Americans, Muhammad is for people in the Middle East, Krishna is for India, and Buddha is for all oriental people. Sadly, that is the misguided view of religion. The truth that when the angel in Luke 2 says, ***"For unto you is born this day in the city of David a Savior, who is Christ the Lord."*** He was not saying a savoir for whites, Americans, Canadians, and European or even man or woman. Christ is the savoir of the world. He loves everyone equally. As Santa has no sense of bias neither does Christ. Jesus loves everyone equally. There is nothing we can do to make God love us any more or any less. As this season rolls forward, take some time and figure out how to love with no bias like Jesus.

GOD IS PRESENT IS THE PRESENT!

Pastor Jeff England | Counseling Pastor

"*Where shall I go from your Spirit? Or where shall I flee from your presence? If I ascend to Heaven, you are there. If I make my bed in Sheol, you are there! If I take the wings of the morning and dwell in the uttermost parts of the sea, Even there your hand shall lead me, and your right hand shall hold me. If I say, "Surely the darkness shall cover me, and the light about me be night," Even the darkness is not dark to you; the night is bright as the day, for darkness is as light with you*" (Psalms 139:7-12).

David took a moment to contemplate God's incredible knowledge of him both inwardly and externally. He exclaims that even the darkness, which includes our thoughts, feelings, and attitudes, is as light to God. He is not contained and cannot be limited in His presence or availability. What if there was one person who knew every thought, feeling, and attitude you ever conceived? Is there any person in your life with whom you would not feel extreme shame if at all times they wholly knew your mind and heart? Probably not. We often ignore the fact that God does know it all! Even though we can choose to forget God's omniscience, it is unavoidable.

This is possibly the most difficult trait of God for us to comprehend: He is everywhere at all times completely unlimited by time or space. Why should He be restrained by the concepts of time and space when He Himself created them? I chuckle when I think about our frustration when we struggle with trying to be in two places at once. We are always late to one or miss the other. Not God. Lewis Sperry Chafer points out in his volumes on Systematic

Theology that if God was anything short of 100% present in 100% of all universes, He could not be God.

The fact that God is always present in every situation, with full knowledge of our every thought, emotion, and weakness is a wonderful gift. He understands our humanness; therefore, we need not let the enemy succeed in his efforts to imprison us with fear, guilt, resentment, and shame. God wants us to use His presence as a foundation for strength and perseverance.
Moses understood the value of God's constant presence. In Exodus 33:15, he made it clear that he was not going to take a single step without God. God told Moses in verse 14 that, *"...My presence shall go with thee, and I will give you rest."* The word "rest" in Hebrew means "Comfortable, quiet rest".

Wow! Not only is God promising us that He will always be there through all of our struggles and hurts, but also that in His presence we will find comfort and rest.

For years, I have heard people who are hurting tell me that they cannot feel God's presence. I too have felt this in my own life, and there have been many times in which I have wished God had skin. When one of these times invade your life, take a moment to look around you and remember the earthly and tangible evidence that we do have of God's presence. We have witnessed God's presence through lives and hearts that have been changed. We see Him in the beauty of our children, the wonder of nature and animals, the sun, moon, and stars. In those moments when you feel so alone, remember the truth that David and Moses understood. He is there, He knows your pain, and He wants to give you rest and comfort. Believe God is present and pursue His presence. Focus on what you know He has done in your life and in the lives of others. Be humble enough to examine your own heart to see if you are bound by a sin or attitude that is hindering His desire to be intimate with you. Praise Him in thought or through music. Enmesh yourself in Scripture. These are but a few ways to invite God's presence into our lives and overcome the loneliness we sometimes feel when struggles appear to be overwhelming.

I hope that this Christmas season provides you with some time for quiet, comfortable rest with loved ones. As we celebrate the incredible present God gave us in Jesus, let us also celebrate the fact that in every aspect of our lives, HE IS PRESENT!

"And the Lord, he it is that doth go before thee: he will be with thee, he will not fail thee, neither forsake thee: Fear not, neither be dismayed" (Deuteronomy 31:8).

GOD IS PRESENT

Philip Piasecki | Worship Leader

T he holiday season is one that can bring both great joy and great sorrow. For many families, it is a time to gather together, spend time with one another, and encourage one another. Unfortunately, for many others, it is a time where the people who are not present become much more magnified. Possibly it is a family member who has passed away, a relationship that has ended, or bridges that have been burned between friends or family members. When everyone is gathered together, it is much more apparent as to those who are missing. When I spent some time thinking about the idea of "God's Present" the phrase "God is present" kept coming into my mind. During a season where it is very easy to start to focus on who is not present in our life, the phrase "God is present" has become such an encouragement for me, and I hope it can be for you as well.

The truth that God is present in our lives can be found throughout Scripture. Matthew 1:23 says, *"'Behold, the virgin shall conceive and bear a son, and they shall call his name Immanuel' (which means, God with us)."* Jesus' name tells us that He is God incarnate! God sent His Son so that He could live in the midst of His people, and eventually give His life on a cross to make a way for salvation. When we have given our lives to Christ, we can know that God is with us in every situation. Psalm 46:1-2 says, *"God is our refuge and strength, a very present help in trouble. Therefore we will not fear though the earth gives way, though the mountains be moved into the heart of the sea."* When we are going through times of trouble, we can rest in the fact that God is our refuge and our strength. The Scripture says that He is a very present help. We do not follow a God that watches us from afar, not interested in what is happening in our

91

lives. We follow a God that is present in the midst of our every circumstance. No matter what is going on, He is there to help calm the storm. He loves us enough to give us strength in the midst of every situation.

John 14:16-18 says, *"And I will ask the Father, and he will give you another Helper, to be with you forever, even the Spirit of truth, whom the world cannot receive, because it neither sees him nor knows him. You know him, for he dwells with you and will be in you. I will not leave you as orphans; I will come to you."* When Jesus physically left this earth, He promised to send a helper. Christ promised that He would not leave us as orphans. He sent us His Holy Spirit to dwell inside of us so that He could be with us at all times. When you feel like no one is there for you, when you feel hopeless in your current situation, know that God is present in the center of the storm with you. He loves you; the Holy Spirit will guide and direct you, and we just need to trust Him.

God IS present.

GOING BEYOND SALVATION

Jared Bruder | Growth Intern

"*A nd an angel of the Lord appeared to them, and the glory of the Lord shone around them, and they were filled with great fear. And the angel said to them, Fear not, for behold, I bring you good news of great joy that will be for all the people. For unto you is born this day in the city of David a Savior, who is Christ the Lord. And this will be a sign for you: you will find a baby wrapped in swaddling cloths and lying in a manger*"* (Luke 2:9-12). Christmas is the time of year we celebrate the birth of our Savior Jesus Christ. Jesus lived a perfect life, died on the cross, and rose again paying the penalty for our sins bringing salvation to you and me.

Salvation from the penalty of our sin is an absolutely amazing gift, but Christ has given us so much more beyond salvation. Romans 5 explains several other gifts beyond salvation that Jesus brought to man. Throughout Romans 5, we see that Jesus has brought us peace with God, access to God, hope, and He has even given us the Holy Spirit.

Romans 5:1 says, *"Therefore, since we have been justified by faith, we have peace with God through our Lord Jesus Christ."* Along with salvation, Jesus has made us at peace with God. We are no longer enemies of God. Romans 5:2a says, *"Through him we have also obtained access by faith."* We now have access to God through Jesus Christ. Continuing on in the passage Romans 5:3-4 says, *"Not only that, but we rejoice in our sufferings, knowing that suffering produces endurance, and endurance produces character, and character produces hope."* Through Jesus, we can endure our trials, and thus it produces hope. Finally, Romans 5:5 says, *"And hope does not put us to shame, because God's love has been poured into our hearts through the Holy Spirit who has been given to us."* We see through this passage that Jesus has brought so much more than salvation from hell.

Remember we do not deserve any of this including salvation from hell. Jesus did not have to die for us, but He did because He loves us. Jesus could have stopped at bringing salvation from hell, but He loved us and brought even more than that. Jesus brought us peace with God, access to God, hope, and the Holy Spirit. All of these gifts we have been given allow us to live a life pleasing to God. All we must do is accept and use these gifts in our life. Spend time with God, hope in God, allow the Holy Spirit to work in your life, and always remember Christ died for us. The least we could do is live for Him.

5

A New Resolution

Pastor Scott Johnson

E very year on January 1, many people set new goals, or resolutions for the upcoming year; things that they want to improve on. It is not uncommon for these goals to revolve around finances, and how to make more money, save more money, and spend less. Often, the new goals are about being a better spouse, parent, or friend. Not surprisingly, though, the most common New Year's resolutions are centered on weight loss and overall physical fitness.

We can probably all agree on some level, that these are good things to work on, and we all need improvement on at least one of those areas. However, are these the most important things in our life? Is there something that deserves more attention?

I Timothy 4:8
"For while bodily training is of some value, godliness is of value in every way, as it holds the promise for the present life and also the life to come."

Not everybody makes a New Year's resolution. I know many may find it silly to take part in a tradition that tells you to make changes just because it is the first day of the year. No matter what side you fall on, there are definitely benefits to looking at yourself and evaluating what things need to change, no matter what day of the year it is. For a believer in Jesus, it is vitally important to understand that there is always a step to take to grow close to Christ in our daily lives.

David wrote a passage that can be a great starting point for a spiritual renewal. It is a great place for us to begin the evaluation process. Certainly, it is not an exhaustive list of things to improve on, but a few simple things for us to ask God in prayer. Let's examine David's requests.

Psalm 51:10-12
"Create in me a clean heart, O God, and renew a right spirit within me. Cast me not away from your presence, and take not your Holy Spirit from me. Restore to me the joys of your salvation, and uphold me with a willing spirit."

1. Create in me a clean heart and a renewed spirit.

Jeremiah 17:9-10
"The heart is deceitful above all things, and desperately sick; who can understand it? 'I the Lord search the heart and test the mind to give every man according to his ways, according to the fruit of his deeds.'"

What is so different about the message the world teaches?

_____

_____

_____

What do we need to understand about our desires?

_____

_____

_____

2. Draw me close to you, and let me be Spirit led.

Galatians 5:16, 22-26

16 *"But I say, walk by the Spirit, and you will not gratify the desires of the flesh.*

22 *But the fruit of the Spirit is love, joy, peace, patience, kindness, goodness, faithfulness,* 23 *gentleness, self-control; against such things there is no law.* 24 *And those who belong to Christ Jesus have crucified the flesh with its passions and desires.* 25 *If we live by the Spirit, let us also keep in step with the Spirit.* 26 *Let us not become conceited, provoking one another, envying one another."*

How is vs. 16 related to our first prayer above? _____

_____

_____

_____

How can we keep from acting out on what our flesh wants to do?

_____

_____

_____

Verses 24-25 speak of those that belong to Jesus. What must be evident in the lives of those who claim this? _____

_____

_____

_____

What does walking in the Spirit look like to you? _____

_____

_____

_____

3. Help me remember what I have been saved from

Ephesians 2:1-9

"And you were dead in the trespasses and sins 2 in which you once walked, following the course of this world, following the prince of the power of the air, the spirit that is now at work in the sons of disobedience— 3 among whom we all once lived in the passions of our flesh, carrying out the desires of the body and the mind, and were by nature children of wrath, like the rest of mankind.[4 But God, being rich in mercy, because of the great love with which he loved us, 5 even when we were dead in our trespasses, made us alive together with Christ—by grace you have been saved— 6 and raised us up with him and seated us with him in the heavenly places in Christ Jesus, 7 so that in the coming ages he might show the immeasurable riches of his grace in kindness toward us in Christ Jesus. 8 For by grace you have been saved through faith. And this is not your own doing; it is the gift of God, 9 not a result of works, so that no one may boast. 10 For we are his workmanship, created in Christ Jesus for good works, which God prepared beforehand, that we should walk in them."

What was a believer's past? _____

_____

_____

How does our past relate to the first two prayers we discussed?

_____

_____

_____

We were saved because of what? _____

_____

_____

Now that we are saved, what is our purpose? _____

_____

_____

_____

Maybe you have already made a New Year's resolution, and maybe you did not. I want to encourage you to spend time in prayer and reflect on what we discussed. Let the scripture we reviewed remind us of what our focus ought to be. It does not have to be January 1. We can always benefit from prayer and meditation on God's Word.

WORKING FAITH

Jared Bruder | Growth Intern

When I was younger, my brother and I both loved being active. There came a point in my life where my brother's passion and my passion took totally different directions. My brother began training and competing in strongman competitions, and I began running marathons. Both of our training required intense workouts and great dedication. After years of competing, I can say that I am a marathon runner, and my brother can say that he is a strong man competitor. We can both say this because we have the actions to back up what we say. I can produce a wall of race medals, and my brother can simply flex his biceps and you know we are telling the truth.

Our faith in God should be the same way. We must be able to produce actions that back up what we say. The Bible says in James 2:18, *"But someone will say, 'you have faith and I have works.' Show me your faith apart from your works, and I will show you my faith by my works."* Our actions will always speak louder than our words. It is important that we do not only claim the name of Christ with words and never actually have actions to back up that claim. Our works will prove our faith. James 2 goes on and uses Abraham as an example of this concept. Abraham's actions, when he did what God commanded him, proved his faith. It was much more than Abraham simply saying he believed God; his actions proved he believed God.

As we enter this New Year, our actions must back up what we say. If you claim to be a follower of Christ, your actions need to back that up. If you claim to read your Bible regularly, you should actually be reading your Bible regularly. To a world that is dying and in need of the saving grace of Jesus, our actions toward them should bring them closer to a saving knowledge of Jesus and not push them away. Many Christians claim to love people yet they push those people, they claim to love away from Jesus. This year let your actions speak louder than your words. Serve Christ with your works and not just your mouth.

OUT WITH THE OLD AND IN WITH THE NEW

Jared Bruder | Growth Intern

This is the year! The year 2017 is the year I will hold to my resolutions and be the best I can. Resolutions spanning from eating less fast food to spending more time reading my Bible. I refuse to be held down by what is behind me. This year I will do better!

Sound familiar? This is my plan for 2017. We have all been there ready to take on the New Year and better ourselves. We spend the first few weeks rocking out our resolutions but soon fall back into our old habits. All of that is past. I refuse to let 2017 be the same as all those other years! I will stick with it!

I want to encourage you as you stick with all the resolutions you have made to add one more to the list. Spend this year getting to know God better. Philippians 3:13-14 says, ***"Brothers, I do not consider that I have made it my own. But one thing I do: forgetting what lies behind and straining forward to what lies ahead, I press on toward the goal for the prize of the upward call of God in Christ Jesus."*** Spend this year pressing toward God.

Pressing towards this goal is accomplished through a few simple tasks. First is simply to talk to God. God has given us the gift of being able to talk to Him. If you want to know God better and know what He wants for your life, you need to talk to Him. The next step is to read your Bible. God not only has given us the gift of talking to Him, but He has also given us His Word.

Many spend their time looking back on their life and say, "I wish I had begun serving God earlier in life. I feel like I have wasted my life." Do not be held down by what is behind. As long as there is breath in your lungs, you can press toward the goal. With this New Year, whether you have just begun serving God, or you have been serving God for a long time, do more this year. Allow God to use you like never before. Press towards the goal this year. Pray more, read more, and do more.

WHAT ARE YOU RUNNING TO?

Christopher Blodgett | Student Ministry Intern

"Do you not know that in a race all the runners run, but only one receives the prize? So run that you may obtain it." 1 Corinthians 9:24

Eat healthier, exercise more, lose weight, stop smoking, get a better job, etc. These are all New Year's resolutions that we have all heard someone say in the last couple of years. These are all things physical. How come we do not hear, read my Bible more, grow deeper with God, or attend church consistently? These are all things to help grow our spiritual relationship with God. Our relationship with God should be more important than looking good physically or making more money. Yet we still worry so much more about these things. It is time for us as a church to set our minds on an eternal perspective, instead of making our life so complicated and just worry about ourselves. We need to simplify our life and center it more towards the cause of Christ.

It is not bad to try to do those things in our life, and there is nothing wrong with trying to better ourselves physically, but often we let that stuff consume our lives. When we find ourselves thinking these selfish thoughts constantly, then we find ourselves straying away from God and tiptoeing towards idolatry. The Bible clearly states that we need to live our lives for Christ, and what better way to do this than by focusing our minds on Christ. We can find so much more pleasure in Jesus that we can in ourselves. Sometimes it may not be easier to focus all of our thoughts on Christ but to do that we need to discipline ourselves towards Christ. It becomes more natural to focus those thoughts when we are fully invested in Him with our thoughts and actions.

There are 24 hours in a day, which equates to 1,440 minutes. How many minutes a day do you actually spend praying, thanking God, or deepening your relationship with Him? Do you spend more time looking in the mirror fixing your hair than you do reading God's Word?

This week how can you redirect your goals away from yourself and more towards Christ?

PUTTING IN THE WORK

Christopher Blodgett | Student Ministry Intern

I was getting ready for my senior year of high school on the hockey team. We had optional summer training three days a week every week for the whole summer. Being the big bad senior, I decided I would much rather enjoy my last high school summer than go to summer training. Months later, I stepped on the ice for my first practice of the season, and within the first five minutes I was winded and puking on the bench from being so out of shape. I sat there on the bench and watched the rest of the team enjoy practice while I was kicking myself for skipping summer training.

Although this may seem like a silly story, we often find ourselves in similar situations in our relationship with God. Our relationship with God is not a one-sided relationship. We cannot just expect to magically become closer to Christ by doing nothing. As followers of Christ, we are to follow God's Word. Throughout the New Testament, we can see through many different stories about the consequences of not listening to God's Word and the blessing of following His Word.

In the book of James, we read a letter that he writes expressing his concern for Christians who were scattered due to persecution. The purpose of his letter was to encourage the new Christians to stray away from ungodly behavior and to follow Christ. James directly tells us in James 1:19-27 that we need to be listening to God's Word and practice what it says. Verse 22 says, ***"But be doers of the word, and not hearers only, deceiving yourselves."***

What can you do to grow closer to Christ? We can gear our thoughts and actions towards Christ. We can pray for more of a desire to know God through the ways we listen, communicate, and focus on God in our everyday lives. We can set our hearts and minds towards the cause of Christ, setting our goals to become more like Christ every day.

OUT OF THE DARKNESS

Michael Young | Student Ministry Intern

W hen I was younger, I did this really weird thing during the night. Only when it was completely dark and it was nearly impossible to see anything in front of you. I would want to get a glass of water, but I would not allow myself to use any light or be able to see. The goal was to get the glass of water by getting through my house without seeing at all, smoothly. From my room, I would have a couple turns, a flight of stairs, couple of hallways, and the mystery of objects being left out along the way. For some reason, I just wanted to see if I could achieve a glass of water without touching anything or running into a wall. The game would always end up with the same outcome. I would either misjudge how far I can walk and fumble around the blank wall looking for a doorknob thinking it is a door, or I would stub my toe on something left out. It was a constant game I played random nights that I would wake up thirsty. There was another issue I had every time I played. By the time I got downstairs to the fridge, I would be totally caught up in this game and I would forget my original goal/purpose for coming down in the first place.

I am reminded of one of my favorite passages of all time. Elijah was called to help the nation of Israel and get rid of Ahab, the king of Israel. In a series of awesome events, Elijah was doing what he was called to do. He challenged Ahab's god Baal, killed all their prophets, and then was perusing Ahab. Then something crazy happened. Ahab's wife Jezebel threated Elijah, and Elijah ran in fear. So in 1 Kings 19:9-18, we see Elijah in a cave 370 miles from where he should be talking to God. God asked him twice why he was here? Elijah lost his goal, his purpose, and what he was meant to do along the way. He was caught up in what had just happened. He ran in fear of some queen. God, being patient and loving, gives Elijah his goal again.

It is very similar to where we are in life at times. We tend to be caught up in something and forget what our goal is. Just losing sight of what God has for us. The good news is that God is loving and patient. Take a moment and reflect on where you are in life right now. Are you following what God has for you or what you have for yourself?

"GREAT" GRANDFATHER

Brett Eberle | Tech Intern

E verybody has that person in their lives that has had a huge effect on who they are today. For me, that person was my great-grandfather. He was one hundred years old when he died in June. He lived through things that most of us could only dream of like the Great Depression and World War II. He told me stories about walking around Pontiac trying to find a job until he wore holes in his shoes, and then filling those holes with cardboard so that he could keep searching. He was not only one of the hardest working men that I have ever met, but he was also one of the godliest. He left a legacy of being a godly man, husband, and father that still drives nearly everyone that he met to be better.

Deuteronomy 5:8-10 says, ***"You shall not make for yourself a carved image, or any likeness of anything that is in heaven above, or that is on the earth beneath, or that is in the water under the earth. You shall not bow down to them or serve them; for I the Lord your God am a jealous God, visiting the iniquity of the fathers on the children to the third and fourth generation of those who hate me, but showing steadfast love to thousands of those who love me and keep my commandments."***

Deuteronomy tells us that all of us will leave a legacy to the generations that follow us, but it is up to us, and the choices that we make, as to what kind of legacy we will leave behind. As the New Year rolls around and you begin to think about how you want to shape the next year, think about the kind of legacy that you want to leave behind. The choices that we make do not just affect us; they will affect our families for years to come. Deuteronomy says that bad legacies of people who hate God will be passed down through three and four generations, but legacies of people who love Him and keep His commandments will go on for thousands of generations. As we set our goals, I challenge you to make your legacy your goal. To leave behind a godly legacy that will bless your family for thousands of generations to come.

My great-grandpa lived for one hundred years and did some of the most amazing things that you could imagine, but the thing that he was most proud of was the fact that his son, his grandkids, and his great-grandkids all knew Jesus. That is the kind of legacy that I want to leave. A legacy of God being so real in my life that everyone I know and everyone that I meet would see Him through me.

6

Reach

Pastor Scott Johnson

The New Year brings many thoughts of new beginnings; the things we want to change, things we should continue doing, and the things we want to make better. As a church body, we would like to revisit the main goals of our ministry and understand the importance of them. Our first step is reach. What exactly does reach mean? It begins with the Great Commission.

Matthew 28:18-20
"And Jesus came and said to them, 'All authority in heaven and on earth has been given to me. 19 Go therefore and make disciples of all nations, baptizing them in the name of the Father and of the Son and of the Holy Spirit, 20 teaching them to observe all that I have commanded you. And behold, I am with you always, to the end of the age.'"

What is commanded here regarding reaching people? _____
_____
_____
_____

Who is Jesus speaking to? _____
_____
_____

Who does this apply to today? _____

_____

_____

_____

Reach is foundational in the church. Without reaching new people for Christ, the church would cease to exist. It is one of the primary purposes of the church. It is extremely important that we strive to accomplish reaching people. The Church exists to glorify God by **reaching the world**, gathering with the saints, and growing in the Word.

In the beginning of Acts, Jesus prepares for His ascension and gives final instruction to His followers. He gives the promise of the Holy Spirit.

Acts 1:6-8

"So when they had come together, they asked him, 'Lord, will you at this time restore the kingdom to Israel?' 7 He said to them, 'It is not for you to know times or seasons that the Father has fixed by his own authority. 8 But you will receive power when the Holy Spirit has come upon you, and you will be my witnesses in Jerusalem and in all Judea and Samaria, and to the end of the earth.'"

What does Jesus expect from His disciples? (Verse 8) _____

_____

_____

_____

How far were the disciples told to reach people? _____

_____

_____

What are some practical ways that we are reaching locally and globally? _____

_____

_____

Do we have the power to reach these people? _____

_____

_____

_____

Reaching people for Christ is at the core of the inauguration of the church. On the day of Pentecost, the Holy Spirit arrived as Jesus had promised, and the world was changed.

Acts 2:1-6, 12

"When the day of Pentecost arrived, they were all together in one place. 2 And suddenly there came from heaven a sound like a mighty rushing wind, and it filled the entire house where they were sitting. 3 And divided the tongues as of fire appeared to them and rested each one of them. 4 And they were all filled with the Holy Spirit and began to speak in other tongues as the Spirit gave them utterance. Now there were dwelling in Jerusalem Jews, devout men from every nation under heaven. 6 And at this sound the multitude came together, and they were bewildered, because each one was hearing them speak in his own language. And they were amazed and astonished....

12 And all were amazed and perplexed, saying to one another, "What does this mean?"

The Holy Spirit came upon the apostles, and they were compelled to tell all who would listen of the amazing Savior they knew personally. They taught and proclaimed Jesus Christ alone. This was the beginning of God's amazing work at the church in Jerusalem.

Peter and the apostles were clear on their message.

Acts 2:37-38
"Now when they heard this they were cut to the heart, and said to Peter and the rest of the apostles, 'Brothers, what shall we do?' 38 And Peter said to them, 'Repent and be baptized every one of you in the name of Jesus Christ for the forgiveness of your sins, and you will receive the gift of the Holy Spirit.'"

When reaching people, what are the key things that they MUST understand? _____

_____

_____

Why is repentance important in receiving Jesus? _____

_____

_____

_____

Peter and the disciples were obedient to the calling of the Holy Spirit. The Bible states that about 3,000 souls were added to the Kingdom of God (Acts 2:41). Their obedience leads to the birth of the church.

The work of the Holy Spirit continued in the early church.

Acts 2:46-47

"And day by day, attending the temple together and breaking bread in their homes, they received their food with glad and generous hearts, 47 praising God and having favor with all the people. And the Lord added to their number day by day those who were being saved."

Reaching lost people for Christ is of the utmost importance. It was in the early church and is today with the Church. We cannot neglect what we have been called to do as followers of Jesus.

What does verse 47 show us about those that need to be reached?

_____

_____

_____

What part can we serve when it comes to reaching the lost? ____

_____

_____

_____

It is important to understand when we discuss reaching people that we know that the church's job does not end there. The Great Commission in Matthew teaches that we are to make disciples. That goes beyond the day they are saved. Our vision is to glorify God through reaching the world, gathering with the saints, and growing in the Word. We will look at the next two steps in our following lessons.

RUN TO WIN

Jared Bruder | Growth Intern

My favorite fitness exercise is running. Yes, it may be hard to believe, but I love running. Most only run when it is a matter of life and death and look at people like me, who simply run for the love of running, as strange. It may be a bit strange, but running is my life. Training for the next 50-mile race, or setting up a plan to accomplish the daunting 100-mile race. Running is not simply something I do; it is part of who I am. You could say I eat, sleep, and breathe running.

In 1 Corinthians 9:22-24, Paul explains that as Christians we should eat, sleep, and breathe the Gospel. Paul states in verse 22, *"To the weak I became weak, that I might win the weak. I have become all things to all people that by all means I might save some."* Winning the lost to Christ was not something Paul did; it was part of who he was. Paul uses an illustration to clarify this concept in verse 24 when he said, *"Do you not know that in a race all the runners run, but only one receives the prize? So run that you may obtain it."* As a runner races to win the prize, we as Christians are to push with all we have to win the lost to Christ. By any means necessary (without sinning), we are to win the lost to Christ.

Sadly, many times we tend to gather at church and pray for the lost to come to Christ, but we never do anything about it. We must go out and make an active effort to win the lost just as Paul did. We must share the same focus as Paul, *"To the weak I became weak, that I might win the weak. I have become all things to all people that by all means I might save some."* Eat, sleep, breathe the Gospel.

In order to eat, sleep, and breathe Gospel it begins with small steps. Just like my running career, I did not just wake up one day and have the ability to run 50 consecutive miles. I started small. I began with competing at the 800-meter (1/2 mile) race in track and slowly built up from there. The same steps must be taken with the Gospel. Start small and build up from there. Invite just one person to church, or share a verse that has impacted you with just one other. Then build up from there, and every time it will become easier to reach out to people with the Gospel. It simply takes practice just like running. So let's begin our Gospel practice.

HOW WILL THEY HEAR?

Jared Bruder | Growth Intern

Some of the best learning experiences in my life have come by way of rhetorical or simple questions. My mother used to ask me rhetorical questions like, "Do you think your room will clean itself?" or my father would ask, "Do you think money grows on trees?" These are simply yet profound questions that changed my whole thought process as a young child. Questions are sometimes used to get our attention. Sometimes simple questions have the greatest influence on us. In the book of Job, Job had lost just about everything, and we find him drowning in self-pity when the Lord speaks to him. The Lord asked Job several questions for example, "Where were you when I laid the foundation of the earth?" All the questions were to show Job how the Lord is in control. The Lord used several simple questions to take Job's focus off his present circumstances and turn his focus to Him.

There are many places in the Bible where God has chosen to use questions to make very emphatic statements. Romans 10:14 reads, *"How then will they call on him in whom they have not believed? And how are they to believe in him of whom they have never heard? And how are they to hear without someone preaching?"* These simple, and yet profound questions should cause us to evaluate our focus. Are we concerned with reaching the lost with the Gospel? What are we doing to better prepare ourselves to reach the lost? Only you can answer all of these questions for yourself.

Understand that if you answer these questions with statements like someone else will reach the lost, someone else can preach, or I am not comfortable with doing that. You must know that there are people you see every day that you may be the last Christian they meet before they enter eternity and stand face to face with God. There may not be someone else that has the chance to share Christ with them. So I ask you the question, *"How are they to believe in him of whom they have never heard?"*

The answer to this question is so simple yet profound at the same time. If they never hear the Gospel, they will not believe. This answer then requires action! We must be sharing the Gospel to those around us. Think of where you would be if no one cared to share the Gospel with you.

REACH OUT BECAUSE HE REACHED OUT

Christopher Blodgett | Student Ministry Intern

"Therefore welcome one another as Christ has welcomed you, for the glory of God." Romans 15:7

It is easy for us to ignore the random people that we see every day because there is a high chance that we will never see them again. Each of us sees upwards of a couple hundred random people throughout any given day. As I was thinking about this, I thought about it in my personal life. When I walk through the grocery store, I sometimes wonder, "I wonder if they are a Christian" or "have they ever heard the Gospel preached?" Chances are many of those people are not Christians or have not heard the Gospel preached. That is such an awful thing to think about, these people have never accepted Jesus in their life and who knows when they could die? It also puts guilt on me. As Christians, we are commanded by Jesus to go out and make disciples in every nation. As a church, we are responsible for sharing the Gospel with these people. We as a church are responsible for the lost. However, many of us have no desire to go out in the world and talk to the people that are lost.

My whole life I have had a heart for the most random people. I could walk up to a stranger and have a conversation with them for hours. It is just what I love to do. I love learning about that person, and quite honestly, it gives me a chance to vent as well. So many times I will find myself talking to a random person and walking away hitting myself in the head because "I never brought Jesus up once in that conversation." Sometimes it can be so hard to just bluntly come out and say, "Hey, you need Jesus!" However, just as we were taught growing up 'actions speak louder than words.' There are so many things that we can do to share the Gospel with someone. We as a church host so many events throughout the year for this exact purpose. You can invite someone to it and not personally have to share the Gospel with him or her. We have outreach events that are planned around sharing the Gospel with the lost. As a church, it is our responsibility to be inviting the lost to these events, because let's face it we all know someone who is lost.

I challenge you this week to invite someone who you know is lost to church on a Sunday or an outreach event coming up. God reached out to us, so don't you think now it is time for you to reach out to someone else?

CLASS IS OVER

Michael Young | Student Ministry Intern

I n college, I had a very interesting experience with a professor. Over the course of a semester, I felt he taught the same lesson in every single class. Somehow, the topic would always be brought back to the same small hint of truth he had to give us. No matter what the topic was that day, it always somehow gravitated back to the same lesson he was shoving down our throats. It was to the point where several classmates started using their attendance passes to skip this class. Okay, confession time, I did it too. The class was called Introduction to Discipleship. He was a short Indian man with a thick accent. I can hear his famous quote perfectly; "Your testimony is your greatest tool for the Gospel!" There was an emphasis on Gospel because of his accent. It took me a while to finally understand what he meant.

However, it is actually biblical truth through which, can be overlooked. If you go to John 4, it is the story of the woman at the well. It is a very famous story and usually read to learn about Jesus being the Living Water, or how He loved everyone. He even loved a Samaritan who the Jews normally hated. The quick summary is this; Jesus came to a woman at a well in Samaria and told her He is the Christ. She, having an ugly past, was blown away at what He told her. She was an outcast and ran to tell the rest of the town of whom she just met. Then we come to this passage.

"Many Samaritans from that town believed in him because of the woman's testimony, 'He told me all that I ever did.' So when the Samaritans came to him, they asked him to stay with them, and he stayed there two days. And many more believed because of his word. They said to the woman, 'It is no longer because of what you said that we believe, for we

have heard for ourselves, and we know that this is indeed the Savior of the world'" (John 4:39-42).

My teacher knew what he was saying. Sometimes we do not know how to be great evangelists. We go thinking I am not a professional no one is going to be saved because of me. You just need to tell your story, nothing fancy at all. The Samaritan was just the bridge connecting people to Jesus. The truth is that God can use anything, and even your story is enough to lead people to Christ. God is the one who does the saving. We just have to be able and ready to used by God.

OVERCOMING FEAR SICKNESS

Michael Young | Student Ministry Intern

A t the start of every high school year, the same thing happened for the first few weeks. Every September in the morning, the same thing happened. It is super embarrassing to admit that this happened but it did. See what happened is that every morning while getting ready for school I threw up. I had real anxiety for school. I could not tell if it was because of the workload, people, or new environment, I just could not figure it out. Every year for four years, the first few weeks, while getting ready for school, I would throw up. It would get annoying if I had eaten breakfast and had to brush my teeth again. The worst is just dry heaving because there was nothing is in my stomach. It just happened every year of high school for a couple of weeks. I was terrified of what was going to happen during school; it felt like an impossible task was coming.

We tend to think reaching people is very similar to how I felt about school. It can appear to be an impossible task. Jesus even warns His disciples of this in Matthew 10:16, ***"Behold, I am sending you out as sheep in the midst of wolves, so be wise as serpents and innocent as doves."*** It is scary to think that Jesus is commanding us to make disciples, to evangelize, and yet, warns us of being surrounded by wolves. Our comfort is whom we are serving and why we are serving Him. Reaching people is not easy, that is made clear but our focus should not be on comfort or ease, rather who we are doing this for. The King, your Savior, and the very person who gave His life to have a relationship with you is the one you want to please.

So when we go out, do not fear. Be wise and be blameless, knowing it will be tough. There will be rejection. They are rejecting Christ, not you.

THE YARD

Brett Eberle | Tech Intern

"*For I was hungry and you gave me food, I was thirsty and you gave me drink, I was a stranger and you welcomed me, I was naked and you clothed me, I was sick and you visited me, I was in prison and you came to me.' Then the righteous will answer him, saying, 'Lord, when did we see you hungry and feed you, or thirsty and give you drink? And when did we see you a stranger and welcome you, or naked and clothe you? And when did we see you sick or in prison and visit you?' And the King will answer them, 'Truly, I say to you, as you did it to one of the least of these my brothers, you did it to me.'"*
Matthew 25:35-40

As somebody who has grown up in church their whole life, I have heard and read these verses many times. Almost every time that I heard, it preached it was always preached with the Great Commission. In the Great Commission, Jesus tells us to go into all nations taking the message of the Gospel. This is where our church's vision is birthed. In the last few years, these verses in Matthew have begun to explode in my life.

I will never forget the first time that I went into a prison yard. I had almost no interest in being there, so the only reason I went was because I was a first-year intern and Pastor Jim said you are going. The basic outline of the show that we do in the yards has been the same since the beginning. We start with a band to draw the crowd, then Rodney comes in and draws them a little closer. By the end of Rodney's show, most of the crowd is totally in and that is when Pastor Jim gets up to speak. After Pastor Jim is done, he gives any of the inmates that would like to pray the opportunity to do so with members of the team that went into the prison. I was twenty years old standing in the middle of a prison yard looking for someone who wanted to be prayed with, and that was when he approached me. I could tell that he was about thirty years old and by looking at him, I could tell that he had been in prison for a while and that he was a bad dude. We began to talk, and as he asked questions about our ministry and our beliefs, I misspoke when answering. I quickly corrected myself but by then he just assumed that I was lying and that everything that I had already told him was a lie. He stormed off, and I never saw him again. I remember thinking to myself "Doesn't he realize that I gave up my weekend to come into a prison and try to show him about Jesus?"

What I did not understand was that this whole idea of reaching the world has nothing to do with us. We are not supposed to be reaching people in hopes of them giving us something in return. Jesus said when you did it to the least of these, which means you share the love of Christ with people who have nothing to offer you in return. We have an incredible Savior who has given us an amazing gift that we in no way, shape, or form deserve. However, we have the ability and the opportunity to share His gift with the world, expecting nothing in return because we already have been given more than we could have ever dreamed.

7

Gather

Pastor Scott Johnson

Reaching the lost for the cause of Christ was the beginning of the church. What is the next step? What should a new believer in Christ do to continue his journey?

_____

_____

_____

"And they devoted themselves to the apostles' teaching and the fellowship; to the breaking of bread and prayers. And awe came upon every soul, and many wonders and signs were being done through the apostles. And all who believed were together and had all things in common." Acts 2:42-44

Describe the word devoted in detail. _____

_____

_____

_____

What is important about fellowship? _____

_____

_____

_____

What is the key ingredient to this church that made it go? _____

_____

_____

_____

After the conversion of the three thousand, the people began to meet. The church was not just a building that they went to each week; it was a group of people who joined to do life together based on their common belief. They lived out their daily lives continually focused on their belief in Jesus. When they believed in Jesus, there was an obvious change in their lives. They began to act differently and associate with people who had the same change in their lives. As a result, the church grew in numbers.

"And day by day, attending the temple together and breaking bread in their homes, they received their food with glad and generous hearts, praising God and having favor with people. And the Lord added to their numbers day by day those who were being saved." Acts 2:46-47

What are the things that you see in this passage that were made important to the church? _____

_____

_____

What was their mindset during this time? _____

_____

_____

_____

What elements do you see in our gatherings that resemble the church in Jerusalem? _____

_____

_____

Compare the last sentence in verse 47 to Matthew 16:18. What is needed to be understood here? _____

_____

_____

As we revisit these principles each year, our goal is to bring our focus back to the things that truly matter in the body of Christ. It is very easy to get side tracked by things that have no eternal significance. We need to focus on why we gather together and why God considers it important.

Hebrews 10:22-25
"Let us draw near with a true heart in full assurance of faith, with our hearts sprinkled clean from an evil conscience and our bodies washed with pure water. Let us hold fast the confession of our hope without wavering, for he who promised is faithful. And let us consider how to stir up one another to love and good works, not neglecting to meet together, as is the habit of some, but encouraging one another, and all the more as you see the Day draw near."

Why do you think we are told not to neglect the gathering together?

_____

_____

_____

What benefit is there to joining together with other believers?

_____

_____

_____

What attributes are seen in this passage that we can take on in
the church? _____

_____

_____

_____

When we join together as believers, we are encouraged in our
purpose. As we look into the New Testament and study the book
of Acts, we can see that the Holy Spirit came down and started
this thing called the Church through the disciples. The disciples
then empowered people like Stephen and Philip. Eventually,
God Himself converts Saul into the body of Christ, and it is
Barnabas who encourages the disciples to trust that Saul has
been converted. Saul's name is changed to Paul, and he starts one
of the most successful ministries in the Bible. As you read all of
these stories that recount each individual's ministry, there is one
common thing to them. They all suffer discouragement, whether
it is ridicule, imprisonment, or even death; but they all also are
encouraged by one another. They write letters to each other to
make sure they stay strong in the cause of Christ, or they make
visits to encourage and keep the churches and believers on track.
It is in the gathering together that they are renewed in the goal
they strive to achieve and to be energized that they are not alone
in this battle for the souls of the masses.

What elements of our gatherings have encouraged you? _____

_____

_____

_____

What things can be forsaken when we neglect to gather with the church? _____

_____

_____

What can be learned from this study in regard to our mindset about gathering with a body of believers in Christ? _____

_____

_____

_____

DON'T NEGLECT IT

Jared Bruder | Growth Intern

W hen I was a child, my parents always were trying to make me do things I did not want to do. They would make me eat the nastiest green things; my mom called them vegetables. They would make me go to bed while the sun was still up. They would not let me sit inside and watch television all day; they forced me to play outside. Maybe you had a similar childhood. Now that I am grown, I understand why my parents made me do those things. They made me do all of those things because they were good for me. I need my vegetables so my body can function properly. I need sleep so my body can grow strong. I need to play outside because it helps me establish healthy active life habits. Now those are all things that I enjoy doing as an adult. I have a steady, healthy diet, I get plenty of sleep, and I spend most of my free time outside running the trails.

Going to church is not much different. I know many people who view gathering together with other believers as a waste of time and not important. However, the Bible tells us in Hebrews 10:24-25, *"And let us consider how to stir up one another to love and good works, not neglecting to meet together, as is the habit of some, but encouraging one another, and all the more as you see the Day drawing near."* God has established gathering together with other believers because it is good for us. Just as eating your vegetables is good for your health, gathering together with believers is good for your spiritual health. We are able to help one another, build each other up, and learn about God together.

When we gather together, we are able to function as the unified body of Christ. We are told in the Bible to gather together.

This allows us to care for one another. Whether it is a church gathering or a small growth community coming together with other believers, it is vital to spiritual health and growth. Just as it is stated in Hebrews, we are to stir up one another to love and good works. Gathering together helps us make each other better. I encourage you not to neglect to meet together. Gather with the believers and make each other better.

SHARPENING ONE ANOTHER

Jared Bruder | Growth Intern

God has made each of us unique. He has given me different life experiences than you, and He has given you different life experiences than me. This means that we see the world differently. If we were both presented with a problem or situation we had to resolve, my answer to the problem might be different from your answer because my life experiences are different from yours.

This is part of God's plan. He made us each different so that we can come together and make each other better. The Bible says in Proverbs 27:17, *"Iron sharpens iron, and one man sharpens another."* The Bible uses the example of iron sharpening iron to help us understand that we need each other. I can make you better, "sharper" as the Bible puts it, and you can make me better, "sharper."

In order for this sharpening to occur, we must come together. The Bible tells us in Hebrews 10:25 not to neglect to meet together. Gathering together with other believers and studying God's Word will bring us to a better understanding of God. When we all come together, we have the opportunity to build each other up and to help each other out with our problems. The Bible is filled with instructions such as in Galatians 6:2 that says, *"Bear one another's burdens, and so fulfill the law of Christ."* This is accomplished through face-to-face interaction, gathering.

This is why we have church in a building where we all come together as the body of Christ and why we have growth communities. Gathering together and growing together as a unified body (church) is not only God's plan but is also an excellent way to learn the Bible and grow as a community.

We need to "sharpen" one another and care for one another. We need to gather together and worship together. If the body of Christ (the church) is divided, it cannot stand. We must be unified, and we must gather together to build that unity. Get involved and "sharpen" one another.

KNOW IT ALL?

Christopher Blodgett | Student Ministry Intern

"On the first day of the week, when we were gathered together to break bread, Paul talked with them, intending to depart on the next day, and he prolonged his speech until midnight." Acts 20:7

A couple of years ago, I saw a friend who I had not seen in some time, and I asked him how he was doing at his new church. His response kind of blew me away. He said, "It's good, I don't really go to church on Sundays anymore because I already know everything." When I heard this, I was appalled. I could not believe that a man who had gone to Bible College and was one of the most involved guys in the church could be saying that. How could he know everything? There is always something to learn from God's Word.

It may be easy for you to sit down and read a book from front to back and understand exactly what the author wants you to know but there is such a drastic difference between a fictional book and the Word of God. Even the smartest most biblically based pastors I know are always talking about how they are learning new concepts and lessons in the Bible. Even after years of trying to figure it out, they are just learning what a specific verse means in the Bible.

In the New Testament, we learn about how often the early church gathered together. *"On the first day of the week, when we were gathered together to break bread, Paul talked with them, intending to depart on the next day, and he prolonged his speech until midnight."* It is so interesting to look back on the disciples from the early church. They were hungry for the Gospel.

147

They always wanted more of it and literally sat in a room for hours to hear Paul preach, yet we get upset when a pastor goes more than 45 minutes.

Often it is so easy for us to read the Bible and skim through the words. It is silly to read a chapter or a book just to say that we read it. I occasionally catch myself reading my Bible without actually obtaining any information. I just read something really quick and skim through the rest of it. I encourage you to start understanding what you read. That may mean you have to read less at one time and take notes, but just understand what you are reading and figure out what God is revealing to you.

GIFTS OF GRACE

Christopher Blodgett | Student Ministry Intern

"For by the grace given to me I say to everyone among you not to think of himself more highly than he ought to think, but to think with sober judgment, each according to the measure of faith that God has assigned. 4 For as in one body we have many members, and the members do not all have the same function, 5 so we, though many, are one body in Christ, and individually members one of another. 6 Having gifts that differ according to the grace given to us, let us use them: if prophecy, in proportion to our faith; 7 if service, in our serving; the one who teaches, in his teaching; 8 the one who exhorts, in his exhortation; the one who contributes, in generosity; the one who leads, with zeal; the one who does acts of mercy, with cheerfulness." Romans 12:3-8

The first time I stepped into a church, I could not help but notice the cliques within the congregation. It was made very clear where I should sit, in the back by myself. Throughout the first couple of months, I started going to more and more events put on by the church. It seemed like at all of the events there were specific groups of people. I never really felt welcomed to the church until one person finally came and got me connected with "their" group of people. This group of people was all 65+, but I did not really care because I had felt welcomed by them. They may not have the exact same interests as me, but it was like a family.

The church is designed with wonderful diversity. There are children, teenagers, young adults, married, elderly people, and much more. The diversity allows for different gifts to be used in the church. It is helpful in the fact that it is well balanced and very welcoming. No matter what age you are, there is a place for you in the church. However, once the church clings tight to these age groups, it takes away from the possibilities that the church can have. We often find the church segregated by these different age groups. We find the young people serving in settings with young people, the elderly serving within the elderly group. However, it does not always have to be this way. There are so many opportunities for the church of Jesus to serve alongside each other. Something that I, a young 21-year-old, have done is start doing hospital visits to the elderly. It is such an amazing opportunity for me to meet people who are in such a different stage of life. It should never be acceptable to say that you do not fit in at your church.

Imagine if the church was unified to the point where when a visitor came for the first time, he or she did not feel obligated to find their age group. When they stepped in, they saw the elderly sitting with the young people and young people sitting with families. Imagine if when it came to serving, everyone served alongside each other, and the older people were teaching the younger newer Christians. Let us all be one body of Christ with no divisions.

WE ARE FAMILY

Michael Young | Student Ministry Director

When I first moved to Chicago for college, it was a very interesting time in my life. It was interesting for the normal reasons like finally moving away, living on my own, and trying to learn about myself. However, one of the most interesting experiences was trying to find a new church. Until this point, I was part of the same church for my entire life, Faith Church. It was the only place that I really understood and knew church to be. It was my family. When I pictured coming home from college and telling stories of everything that happened, it was not to my immediate family. It was to my church. I had to leave that umbrella of everything I knew and shop for a new church. Every weekend was an adventure to find the perfect church for me. I saw a crazy amount of churches, from mega churches to small holes in the wall places, to big name church plants, and even to a place that did not have a name or location. It was an awesome learning time for me.

The issue was tough; going from place to place, I never really knew what I was looking for. One week would have the best speaker and the worst music, so I would not stay. Another week would have communion with real wine, and it was way too hipster for me. Each week I would experience something I did not like or could pick apart to the point I would not want to go, right up to Thanksgiving. Someone on my floor invited me to Thanksgiving dinner with his church. I said sure why not. When we arrived, he told me it was the pastor's house, and the entire congregation would be there. I was a little nervous. When I walked in, it was like going to a family reunion. I was blown away at this. The church welcomed me warmly and wanted to know me. The church was a family, not just on this Thanksgiving event either. I followed up with going to a couple of services, very similar experience. The church was family, and that is what I should have been looking for. The family aspect like my home church had.

When you look at the beginning of the church in Acts 2:42-47, it is more than just the meet and greet deal. Every day they did life together. It was less of an organization or building location but a family. I learned in my college church shopping time that gather is more than coming together for Sundays or events; it is family time. Family time is important, doing life together as the church was meant to do is important. The original church in Acts saw the church as more than just a location or time slot; it was a family. Is the church an event you attend? Or time with your family? Are you making time to gather with your family?

THE PACK

Brett Eberle | Tech Intern

"*And let us consider how to stir up one another to love and good works, not neglecting to meet together, as is the habit of some, but encouraging one another, and all the more as you see the Day drawing near.*" Hebrews 10:24-25

Gatherings have always been a normal part of my life. Since I was born, there are maybe a handful of weekends where I did not attend at least one gathering. Even though my parents stressed the importance of attending a gathering every weekend, I never really understood why it was so important until I was in high school.

I attended Clarkston High School where I played football for the school all four years that I was there. The football field is where I learned why it is so important to gather together. Clarkston's mascot is a wolf. All of the sports teams and the entire student body were taught a theme. That theme was "The strength of the wolf is in the pack, and the strength of the pack is in the wolf." When I was in high school, I only thought this quote applied to the football field, but when I read these verses in Hebrews, I was immediately reminded of these words that my coach had pounded into our heads on the field. I had the privilege of playing with some truly talented kids, but if the other ten guys did not play as hard as they could, it did not matter how good that one kid was. Without the support of the other kids that were on the field with our star player, there was no room for him to do what needed to be done to win the game.

This is how gatherings are supposed to work. We come together as a body of believers to encourage one another. The world that we live in today will try to beat you into the ground, much like the players on the other team tried to do to us. However, with the support of your teammates, your brothers and sisters in Christ, we can accomplish anything for the Kingdom of God.

8

Grow

Pastor Scott Johnson

We have seen how when we reach people, it causes us to gather together in a common bond with the purpose of growing the church. It is an organic process that happens naturally if we are reaching and gathering with the purpose we intended. However true that may be, the 'grow' that we are talking about here is not the growing of the church in size. The 'grow' we are referring to here is the discipleship of each believer. The focus is on the new believer becoming mature in his faith. Jesus put a great deal of emphasis on the process of discipling in His ministry. He specifically called 12 men to come alongside Him and do ministry with Him. He helped them understand what it meant to be a follower of Christ and how it looked to live that out.

Let's go back and look at our main passage in Scripture from where we draw our vision as a church - The Great Commission.

Matthew 28:18-20
"And Jesus came and said to them, 'all authority in heaven and on earth has been given to me. Go therefore and make disciples of all nations, baptizing them in the name of the Father and of the Son, and of the Holy Spirit, teaching them to observe all that I have commanded you. And behold, I am with you always, to the end of the age.'"

What is the specific command given by Jesus here? _____

_____

_____

_____

What does it mean to be a disciple? _____

_____

_____

_____

What does the Great Commission have to do with spiritual growth? _____

_____

_____

It is interesting to note that those that follow Jesus are told to make disciples of others. It is imperative that we cannot be satisfied with the initial acceptance of Christ. When someone believes in Jesus and is saved, there ought to be a desire to know more about the God who saved you. Just as that was true in our own lives, it is our job as the church to teach others the importance of a growing relationship with Jesus.

When the church started and began to grow, the church had much ministry to do. The apostles alone could not handle the load. Were these just random men? Certainly not. The apostles followed Jesus example of pouring into another with the intent of discipling them toward the life in Christ they were meant to have.

"Therefore, brothers, pick out from among you seven men of good repute, full of the Spirit and of wisdom, whom we will appoint to this duty. But we will devote ourselves to prayer and to the ministry of the word. And what they said pleased the whole gathering, and they chose Stephen, a man full of faith and of the Holy Spirit, and Philip, and Prochorus, and Nincanor, and Timon, and Parmenas, and Nicolaus, a proselyte of Antioch. These they set before the apostles, and they prayed and laid their hands on them. And the word of God continued to increase, and the number of disciples multiplied greatly in Jerusalem, and a great many of the priests became obedient to the faith." Acts 6:3-7

Why do you think these men were chosen? _____

_____

_____

_____

Why were these men needed? _____

_____

_____

_____

What continued to happen within the church? _____

_____

_____

_____

This passage shows the first 'passing of the torch' to the next generation of ministers of the Gospel. As you continue to read through the book of Acts, not only does the new generation start a fire for the cause of Christ, but the old generation, the disciples, are continually in contact with them to help encourage them and teach them in the ways they should be going.

Eventually, Saul is converted to the cause of Christ, and his name is changed to Paul. He works alongside of men like Barnabas, Silas, and Timothy. He ministers alongside these men as they grow in their walk together all the while ministering to the unbelievers. As his ministry continues, we read his many letters in the New Testament that he writes to the churches he had a hand in starting. He instructs them in the ways they should be living in their walk with Christ. He reprimands when it is needed. He encourages when struggles come. He praises when they are doing what they should and produce fruit for the Kingdom of God. He is discipling all of these churches with the intent of growing each believer in their walk with Christ. As they grow in Christ, they can begin to disciple new believers and gives them the ability to give an answer when they are asked about their belief in Christ. The answers they are able to give can bring conversion and change in another's life and therefore causes the church to grow. Both forms of 'grow' are directly intertwined.

In what ways are you growing spiritually? _____

_____

_____

_____

What ways can you improve when it comes to spiritual growth?

_____

_____

_____

How can you help someone else with his or her growth? _____

_____

_____

_____

FAILURE TO GROW

Jared Bruder | Growth Intern

As a child, I was not growing like other children my age. My parents began to realize something was wrong, so they took me to the doctors. When I was five years old, I was diagnosed with what is called Congenital GHD (Growth Hormone Deficiency). This means that though my body was producing growth hormone, it was not producing enough for me to grow at a normal rate. When I was five years old (when I was diagnosed), I was the average size of a two and a half-year-old. At this point, I began growth hormone therapy. This therapy consisted of daily injections of a synthetic growth hormone so that my body would begin to grow. It was not until I was a freshman in high school that I was finally within the normal size for my age.

Many Christians have a growth deficiency when it comes to their spiritual growth. The Corinthian church had this problem with some of its members. In 1 Corinthians 3:1-2 Paul says, *"But I, brothers, could not address you as spiritual people, but as people of the flesh, as infants in Christ. I fed you with milk, not solid food, for you were not ready for it. And even now you are not yet ready."* This problem still permeates our churches today. We have Christians that have a failure to grow spiritually.

It is time for some spiritual growth therapy. We are instructed in 2 Peter 3:18, *"But grow in the grace and knowledge of our Lord and Savior Jesus Christ. To him be the glory both now and to the day of eternity. Amen."* The first step in spiritual growth therapy is to begin increasing your knowledge of God. This is accomplished through daily doses of Bible study. This should be done alone and in association with a growth community. We need to be striving to know God better so that what was said of the Corinthians will not be said of us. Let us strive to not be babes in Christ but rather let us grow in the Word. Spiritual growth is important to strengthen the body of Christ (Church). Do not get diagnosed with spiritual growth deficiency. Get in the Word and grow.

DON'T JUST TALK THE TALK

Jared Bruder | Growth Intern

L et's say one day you decide you wish to be a bodybuilding legend. I tell you I can train you because I am an expert in all things bodybuilding. I have been bodybuilding for most of my life, and at points, it feels that is all I do is lift weights. If you train like me, you will become a bodybuilding legend guaranteed. We meet up for our first training session where you find out I am in fact a small-framed distance runner. At this point, you would call me a liar because I said I was a bodybuilder, but my actions say I am a distance runner.

That would be totally unacceptable in that situation for me to claim to be something I am not, but churchgoers do this all the time. Some claim to be a Jesus follower, but their actions tell a very different story. Part of our growth as a believer and follower of Jesus is our works must match our talk. This issue is addressed in the book of James that states, *"But someone will say, 'you have faith and I have works.' Show me your faith apart from your works, and I will show you my faith by my works"* (James 2:18). Our works validate our speech and sometimes even speak louder than our speech. We must come to the point in our life of following Jesus where our actions match what we say.

Those who do not believe will watch how you act before they ever listen to what you have to say. For this reason, Jesus said in John 13:35, *"By this everyone will know that you are my disciples, if you love one another."* It has been said of old, "Preach the gospel, and if necessary, use words." The way we live our lives is very important. If we claim to be a Jesus' follower, our actions must show that we indeed follow Jesus.

Being a Christian is not so much what you say but what you do. Live your life in such a way that you do not have to tell those around you that you are a Christian. They will already know you are because of the way in which you live your life. Your actions will speak, and then your words will be even stronger. Do not just say you follow Jesus; instead you should actually follow Him.

TEAMWORK MAKES THE DREAM WORK

Christopher Blodgett | Student Ministry Intern

"If one member suffers, all suffer together; if one member is honored, all rejoice together."
1 Corinthians 12:26

Reading this verse makes me think about the time I broke my ankle. I decided it would be a great idea to jump off a stage at a youth event to pump up the kids. What I did not know is that right in my landing zone there was a pile of footballs. So here I am running and leaping off the stage as high as I could, coming down to land on the footballs. I instantly knew something was wrong with my ankle. I was taken to the hospital, and the rest is history. For the next eight weeks of my life, I could not put full pressure on my ankle, let alone walk normally. The same way Paul tells us, ***"If one member suffers, all suffer together..."*** Since my ankle was hurt, my whole body had to suffer from it. I could not do any physical activity. I sat on the couch, eating junk food, and watching way too much TV. All because of one broken bone in my body, now my whole body has to suffer.

Paul is talking about the church body in this context. Christ and His church form one body of believers. All Christians are a part of this body. Just like our physical bodies, every part of this body that Paul talks about, every member, has a specific function and duty. Each member of the body needs the other parts to function. Each member of the body needs to be close to each other and in communication with others. Jesus tells us we should be closely attached through love. Each member should also work well with the other parts of the body because each member is dependent on the other. The Body is made up of many people, and there are so many different skill sets in this body. I encourage you to figure out what the skill set that God gave you is and use it to strengthen the body.

WALK FORWARD

Michael Young | Student Ministry Intern

Growing up in a church, I was very fortunate to have seen many crazy things happen in my few years. I have seen amazing things such as loads of people being saved, baptized, and giving their lives to Christ. I have witnessed weird things like cheesy, lame, skits causing kids to chant Jesus from the top of their lungs. Even seeing a few youth leaders go into ministry in a completely different state or country for the sake of Christ. Being able to serve people in other countries, God can do some awesome and powerful things.

However, a sadness and brokenness can be found as well. In high school, I was a witness to one of the saddest things you will find in a church. An event that shook the youth group and caused a lot of distress. A friend of mine decided to leave the faith. He just walked away from everything he was a part of and hated God. I know what you are thinking, "What would cause someone to do such a thing?" It was something I personally could not wrap my head around. It was the question all of us had at the time while this was happening. The answer is brutal. He was an infant believer and never grew in his faith since being saved.

Ephesians 4:14 says, *"So that we may no longer be children, tossed to and fro by the waves and carried about by every wind of doctrine, by human cunning, by craftiness in deceitful schemes."*

The warning is here; the world is trying to hurt us and is trying to destroy every one of us no matter what. We live in a broken, messed up world. It wants to trick us and deceive us; that is the warning in Ephesians. Yet, how we combat this issue is growing and maturing in the Word. We should be taking steps in the right direction in our walk towards Christ. If we do nothing from the time we are saved, we are infant believers, never growing spiritually. So the question becomes are you taking your walk seriously? Are you working to grow in your walk with Christ? Are you growing in His Word? This is not meant to scare but instead encourage believers to equip themselves for what is to come.

WAVE RUNNER

Michael Young | Student Ministry Intern

I do not recall when I learned how to do many things whether it was riding a bike, whistling, tying my shoes, etc. Most people can usually remember when they finally discovered the trick in how to do these things. All of those to me have become a blur besides swimming. Swimming was important in hot summer days, and I needed to learn. I recall being at a hotel with my family and standing by the pool by myself while my parents helped my brother. This pool was beautiful; at the end of the pool, the wall edged with rocks and was topped with a waterfall trickling down into a wavy deep end. The shallow part of the pool had jets here and there scattered about. Just a beautiful indoor pool with all the toys needed to make a child go crazy. For some reason, I had the wild idea that the time to learn how to swim is right now. I jumped in, not thinking I should start slow, maybe in the shallow end first, no just jumped in. I am told my father heard me screaming and drowning way further from the edge of the pool where I had jumped, rather he found me under the waterfall at the complete opposite end. What happened was where I had jumped there was a jet that pushed my small three or four-year-old body way out to the deep end. It is funny looking back at it now, yet it is very similar to our Christian lives.

Sad truth is we live in a broken world of confusion and pain. It is always trying to hurt and trick us in every possible way. It will try to throw us around and deceive us. Ephesians 4:14 says, ***"So that we may no longer be children, tossed to and fro by the waves and carried about by every wind of doctrine, by human cunning, by craftiness in deceitful schemes."***

This passage warns us of the world's schemes to hurt us. However, instead of just drowning like infants, we are to grow and train in Christ. We need to be studying His Word, growing, and developing our lives for Christ. You need to ask yourself if you are growing in the Word. I told that story because it is the state of new believers in the world we live. They will be thrown around and tossed by the waves or tricks of the enemy.

A LION TAMER

Brett Eberle | Tech Intern

"*Be sober-minded; be watchful. Your adversary the devil prowls around like a roaring lion, seeking someone to devour.*" 1 Peter 5:8

As I dug through my Bible looking for a verse that perfectly fit into this devotional, 1 Peter 5:8 kept popping into my head. The Devil hates you and would like nothing more than to rip your life to shreds. This is especially true once you become a follower of Christ. What I forgot as a young believer was this idea of the Devil prowling. It means the Devil is waiting for you to make a mistake, no matter how small, so that he can pounce on and use against you.

I was in a relationship as I began my college career and the Devil used that relationship to very nearly destroy my bond with my parents and ultimately my life. Looking back at the mistakes that I made, I realized that there was a single moment that the Devil grabbed. That moment was when I took my eyes off what God wanted me to do, and I put them on what she wanted. The story only goes downhill from there. I rarely attended church, I was not growing in the Word, and I had almost no relationship with my parents. When we broke up, I was left broken, and I felt that I had nowhere to turn. However, with the help of some of my Pastors, I ran to the Bible, and I ran back to God.

As I truly began to grow in God's Word, I learned how to deal with my brokenness. I learned how to fight the loneliness, the bitterness, and the resentment that I had in my life. This has become one of the biggest parts of growing in the Word for me. Every time that I slip up and the Devil tries to exploit a weakness,

I run to the Word, and I get a new tool to fight back against this beast who wants nothing more than to destroy me. I will not be destroyed because I have an amazing God who has given me His Word as a tool and a guideline for everything that I have and will go through in life.

9

Back to Reach

Pastor Scott Johnson

Over the past month, we have revisited the vision of the Church. As a church we exist to reach the lost for Christ, to gather together with the saints, and to grow in the Word. We have gone through the points that our church would like to revisit in order to spark a new passion for pursuing these important things of God. Many times, it is just left there. We just focus on the fact that we need to continually pursue God to grow our faith. While this is true, it is not the end all point. So what is next? Are we satisfied when this is accomplished? Certainly not. When a person's life has been transformed by Christ, there ought to be a desire to continue to spread that Good News. After you have been reached, found a church body to gather with, and have grown in your faith, it is now your turn to go back to the reach stage. You are called to be a witness to nonbelievers and reach them for Christ.

Who was the person or people who were most influential in your salvation? _____

_____

_____

Can you think of one person that you know needs to hear about Christ? _____

_____

_____

In what ways does the church do this well? _____

_____

_____

_____

It has been said that the greatest way to learn and grow in a skill is to teach that skill to another person. Perhaps the greatest example of this in the Bible is the apostle Paul. When he was converted, God Himself did the reaching. While Saul was on a quest to persecute more believers, God called him to believe. His encounter with God left him blind. He was told to go to Ananias for his vision to be restored. Ananias had heard of Saul's reputation for persecuting believers, and he was afraid. The Lord calmed Ananias' fears and told him that Saul was the vessel He had chosen and to restore his sight. After Saul's vision had been returned, he was immediately set on his task. Saul's name was changed to Paul. He was a new man.

Acts 9:18-22

18 And immediately something like scales fell from his eyes, and he regained his sight. Then he rose and was baptized; 19 and taking food, he was strengthened. For some days he was with the disciples at Damascus. 20 And immediately he proclaimed Jesus in the synagogues, saying, "He is the Son of God." 21 And all who heard him were amazed and said, "Is not this the man who made havoc in Jerusalem of those who called upon this name? And has he not come here for this purpose, to bring them bound before the chief priests?" 22 But Saul increased all the more in strength, and confounded the Jews who lived in Damascus by proving that Jesus was the Christ.

What were Saul's steps of action?

_____

_____

_____

What was he proclaiming? Why?

_____

_____

_____

Why would the people question what he was saying?

_____

_____

_____

Saul was converted; he sat under the disciples training for 'some days'; and then he began to start the job God had personally given him to do. He began to proclaim Jesus to the lost world. What proceeded were some of the most influential missionary journeys recorded in the Bible. He also was responsible for the continued education of many churches that were reaching the lost for Christ. He is the prime example of what God called us to do in the Great Commission.

Often we hear the need to continue to reach people, but sometimes we do not exactly know how. While Paul was a good example to follow, Peter gives us practical advice about how we go about reaching others. In 1 Peter, he urges the church to reach people by living a life that is honoring to God and to being a light to those around them.

I Peter 2:9-16

9 But you are a chosen race, a royal priesthood, a holy nation, a people for his own possession, that you may proclaim the excellencies of him who called you out of darkness into his marvelous light. 10 Once you were not a people, but now you are God's people; once you had not received mercy, but now you have received mercy. 11 Beloved, I urge you as sojourners and exiles to abstain from the passions of the flesh, which wage war against your soul. 12 Keep your conduct among the Gentiles honorable, so that when they speak against you as evildoers, they may see your good deeds and glorify God on the day of visitation. 13 Be subject for the Lord's sake to every human institution, whether it be to the emperor as supreme, 14 or to governors as sent by him to punish those who do evil and to praise those who do good. 15 For this is the will of God, that by doing good you should put to silence the ignorance of foolish people. 16 Live as people who are free, not using your freedom as a cover-up for evil, but living as servants of God.

What phrases are uniquely used in verse 9? Who is that referring to? _____
_____
_____

What does Peter encourage the church to do? Why?
_____
_____
_____

How should this look in an everyday practical way?

_____

_____

_____

Christians strive to seek God's will. What does Peter say is God's will in this passage?

_____

_____

_____

How does this passage change the way you look at or lifestyle as a witness?

_____

_____

_____

Paul gives us an example to emulate, and Peter gives us instructions on how to walk through life as a believer to be a light to nonbelievers. However, the New Testament is full of other examples and instructions on how to do this. Following what the Scripture tells us is the beginning of bringing it back to reach. If you know Jesus, gather with believers regularly, and are growing in the Word; seek the Lord on how to share the love of Christ with others. Who has God put around you that needs to know the truth of Jesus? Live as servants of Jesus.

TEACHING HOW TO TEACH

Jared Bruder | Growth Intern

T here are people that go to college and major in teaching. This basically means that they go to college to be taught how to teach. I am one of those people. Teaching was my minor in college. In my teaching classes, the goal was to teach me how to teach others. Parents have the same goal when raising their children. They teach them, hopefully, how to be good parents so that they can one day teach their children how to be good parents and so the process will continue.

The Christian life brings with it the same purpose. We reach the lost, they gather with the believers, they grow spiritually, and then they are taught how to go back and start the process over again. I had a professor in college that explained this concept by saying we were not to make disciples, but we are to make disciple makers. Jesus did this with His disciples. The final command Jesus gave here on earth was, ***"Go therefore and make disciples of all nations, baptizing them in the name of the Father and of the Son and of the Holy Spirit, teaching them to observe all that I have commanded you. And behold, I am with you always, to the end of the age"*** (Matthew 28:19-20). Jesus commanded His disciples to go make disciples. Jesus had taught them and then He wanted them to teach others.

This process continued down to Paul teaching Timothy and continues even today with you and me. We are to learn the Bible, and we, as Jesus' followers, are to go and teach others. Reaching others with the Gospel and then teaching them how they can reach more is vital to the Christian life. We live in a world dying without God. The more Christians we have that will reach the world, the more people can come to know God just as you and I do. This process does not end: reach, gather, grow, and go back to reach. Let us join to reach this world with the love of Christ.

DUPLICATION

Jared Bruder | Growth Intern

To this point, if you have been keeping up with this devotional book as well as the sermons being preached, you have covered reach, gather, and grow. Now is the time to understand that being a Christian does not end there. The process must be duplicated. We call this step, "Back to reach." This is not simply starting the process over again but, "back to reach" is a step all its own.

"Back to reach" is teaching Christians how to reach others. In the Bible, Paul taught young Timothy, and one of the last instructions Paul gave him was, ***"And what you have heard from me in the presence of many witnesses entrust to faithful men who will be able to teach others also"*** (2 Timothy 2:2). The final instruction was not only to apply what he had been taught, but it also was to teach others what he had been taught. As Christians, we are to do the same.

Many at times feel they are unqualified to teach others. They say that they do not know the Bible well enough, or they do not know what to say. You might be in that mindset right now. Know this; we have all been there at some point. If you do not know where to start, simply start with Salvation. Think back to when you first became a believer. Can you explain to someone how to know for sure that he or she is going to Heaven? If not, here is your first lesson on how to reach others.

THE PLAN OF SALVATION

Romans 3:23 ***"For all have sinned and fall short of the glory of God."***

Sin is anything we think say or do that breaks God's law. This means we are separated from God.

Romans 6:23 *"For the wages of sin is death, but the free gift of God is eternal life in Christ Jesus our Lord."*

Because of sin, we have broken God's law and the penalty (wages) of sin is death. However, Jesus paid that penalty for us, and we are told it is a free gift.

Romans 10:9-10 *"Because, if you confess with your mouth that Jesus is Lord and believe in your heart that God raised him from the dead, you will be saved. For with the heart one believes and is justified, and with the mouth one confesses and is saved."*

Simply and truthfully believe that Jesus' death, burial, and resurrection has paid for your sins, confesses that He is Lord, and you will be saved.

"Lord I believe that you died for me. And I believe that you rose again. I pray right here and now that you would save me from my sins and come into my life and be my God. In Jesus name, I pray. Amen!"

That is how one is saved, and this is how it can be explained. Use this model to reach others and thus complete the process of reach, gather, grow, and then back to reach.

QUICK TO THOUGHT...

Christopher Blodgett | Student Ministry Intern

"*As he passed by, he saw a man blind from birth. 2 And his disciples asked him, 'Rabbi, who sinned, this man or his parents, that he was born blind?' 3 Jesus answered, 'It was not that this man sinned, or his parents, but that the works of God might be displayed in him.'*" John 9: 1-3

Every week during the school year, our church busses in nearly 1,000 kids to our different locations to have a night filled with fun and then present the Gospel to them. Many of these kids are coming from broken, lost households. Most of these kids are missing a parent or both parents; many are involved in drug addiction or other addictions of some sort. This is what we, as a church, would call our outreach group. Most of these are people do not know Jesus Christ. A group of kids this size and this diverse can really start to test our patience. It is so easy for us to expect these kids to live and act how we Christians do. We get this mindset that because we are bringing them to the church building they should not be any problem to us, but often we are so quick to point out a kid's sin and disregard them.

However, this is not at all what Jesus would want us to do. In John 9, we read a story about how Jesus heals a man who was born blind. When Jesus was walking through the city of Jerusalem, he stumbles across a blind man. Right as He sees the blind man Jesus' disciples are quick to ask, **"*Rabbi, who sinned, this man or his parents...?*"** Jesus' disciples quickly came to the conclusion that the only reason this man was blind was because of his sins. Jesus responded to them, **"*It is not that this man sinned, or his parents, but that the works of God might be displayed in him.*"**

So many times in life we are like the disciples, we see an outreach person and quickly pick out their sins, but that is not what we are to do. The reason God has put these people in our lives is to see the good works of God through these people. The struggling, addicted, broken people are all part of Gods wonderful creation, and He is putting them in our life to see God's work, not to judge.

God can work in anyone's life no matter what stage that person is in. There are so many people in our lives that we have pushed away because we think that they are too far gone or that God cannot save them. We know that He sent His Son to die on the cross for ALL of our sins so that then may be forgiven.

Today, think of someone that you have pushed out of your life because you did not think the good works of God could be displayed on him or her. Commit to pray for this person that God may become a part their life, and if you are feeling ambitious try inviting them to some of our outreach events!

SECRET SERVICE

Michael Young | Student Ministry Intern

For my first year of college, I did not go away like most people would or wanted to do. I decided to do my first year online and help serve in the church as much as possible. I received a call one morning from a staff member who asked me, "If I was ready to serve?" I said, "Of course." He told me to be at the church around noon. He called at nine in the morning that left me several hours just to wait. The issue was that I had no clue what we were doing. He never gave me a hint of an idea. Well, time rolled by after a little while and I got to the church ready for this mystery task. I pulled into the parking lot, and he is already in a van ready to drive somewhere. I thought that maybe we are going to the hospital or some event because it is clearly not at the church. That has to be it; my mind was going through ideas. However, as I climbed into the van I looked in the back, and to my surprise, there were gardening tools. My brain could not connect the dots between serving and gardening. This was supposed to be serving. That day I learned serving does not come in a streamlined box, it comes in many shapes and sizes. I spent the entire afternoon gardening someone's yard that was not even home. It was hot and very boring pulling weeds for someone I did not know at all. I learned a lot about serving.

When it comes to serving, it does not always mean one thing. It is not always something you are comfortable with, or you are aware it is needed. Most of the time God works by not telling us what we are supposed to do, which leave us to just walk by faith. Serving is bigger than we can see. We do not know its purpose most of the time. It reminds me of a story in 1 Kings 17. Elijah is called to help the nation of Israel and get rid of the King Ahab. At the very moment Elijah speaks to the king, ravens are feeding him by a brook. It does not make a ton of sense. Elijah was speaking to the king; he had every chance to do something crazy cool. He was called to serve, and then he does the most random things serving the Lord. It is a real practical lesson for us; serving does not always mean being comfortable or knowing what it is. Serving is just what we are called to do.

GET YOUR HANDS DIRTY

Michael Young | Student Ministry Intern

B eing an avid moviegoer, I see many trends. One trend, in particular, is how they depict a certain character type. Look at leaders in movies across the board. Whether it is a king, emperor, gang leader, president, captain, or even business owner, they usually have the same characteristics. They have some fancy lair, castle, house, or whatever it may be. They usually have some look or style that separates them from the rest of the group. They have several followers catering to them, but most of all they do not get their hands dirty. While watching a lot of movies, I notice that the leaders (usually villains) never seem to get their hands dirty. That is, of course, until all easy tricks fail and they have no choice but to get their hands dirty. Then they say a cheesy line like "if you want it done right, you have got to do it yourself." Yet, the point still stands, leaders never get into the grit and grime of day-to-day operations; they are "above it." In the character's background, they have done everything before, but now they have achieved leadership and a place to be proud. Working is beneath them. Their job is to give orders and never to do anything themselves.

Is this the case for you? Have you gotten to a place where serving is beneath you? Are certain jobs you have done in the past just not worthy of your time now? Look at Mark 10:43-45, *"But it shall not be so among you. But whoever would be great among you must be your servant, and whoever would be first among you must be slave of all. For even the Son of Man came not to be served but to serve, and to give his life as a ransom for many."* Jesus tells His disciples that in Christianity the hierarchy will be different. Actually, it is completely upside down from the world. Leaders will be the servants, and no one is above this, even Christ came to serve. Pride can hinder us from this truth. No one is above serving and loving people; leadership will be known for its service. Pride may get in our way, but we are called to serve even when our hands might get dirty.

LOVE SPINS

Brett Eberle | Tech Intern

"Go therefore and make disciples of all nations, baptizing them in the name of the Father and of the Son and of the Holy Spirit, teaching them to observe all that I have commanded you. And behold, I am with you always, to the end of the age." Matthew 28:19-20

You may have noticed that The River's "reach, gather, grow" logo is in a circle and some of you may have even seen the one that spins. There is a purpose for that and it all falls under this idea of "back to reach." Once you have been reached, you will begin to gather with the saints and grow in the word. Then it is time for you to head out into the world and reach people with the same Gospel that grabbed hold of your life.

I realized that God was calling me into ministry about five years ago. When I realized my calling, I jumped into our student ministry with both feet, but there was a problem. A huge number of kids that I was trying to minister to and share the Gospel with came from homes that I could never imagine. I have amazing parents. They have both supported me through everything that I have done my entire life, and they have shown me what living for Christ is supposed to look like. I am more grateful to my parents than I could ever express for the life they have given me. However, it was this life that was making it so difficult for me to share the Gospel with my students.

It was my first year going to camp as a leader, and I was sitting and talking with one of the seventh grade boys who was in my cabin. He told me about his home life, and every word that he said will forever be seared into my brain. I had no idea how to relate to him, I did not know what it meant to deal with divorced and abusive parents. His story nearly broke me on the spot. I remember just sitting there in awe of what I had just heard. The next day I sat down with Pastor Jim and asked him how on earth I could help this young man. I was expecting some hugely deep theological answer, but that was not what I got. His directions were very simple; he said, "You have to love him."

Jesus told us that the greatest commandment is to love God and to love each other. That is what back to reach is all about. It is about spreading the same love of Christ that you received to anyone and everyone that you can. It does not matter where you are from or where they are from, what walk of life they are in or what walk of life you are in. We are called, as followers of Christ, to spread His love to "all nations."

OUR MISSION

Matthew 28:19-20: *"Go therefore and make disciples of all nations, baptizing them in the name of the Father and of the Son and of the Holy Spirit, teaching them to observe all that I have commanded you. And behold, I am with you always, to the end of the age."*

REACH

At The River Church, you will often hear the phrase, "we don't go to church, we are the Church." We believe that as God's people, our primary purpose and goal is to go out and make disciples of Jesus Christ. We encourage you to reach the world in your local communities.

GATHER

Weekend Gatherings at The River Church are all about Jesus, through singing, giving, serving, baptizing, taking the Lord's Supper, and participating in messages that are all about Jesus and bringing glory to Him. We know that when followers of Christ gather together in unity, it's not only a refresher it's bringing life-change.

GROW

Our Growth Communities are designed to mirror the early church in Acts as having "all things in common." They are smaller collections of believers who spend time together studying the word, knowing and caring for one another relationally, and learning to increase their commitment to Christ by holding one another accountable.

The River Church
8393 E. Holly Rd. Holly, MI 48442
theriverchurch.cc • info@theriverchurch.cc

BOOKS BY THE RIVER CHURCH